Skill-Builders

Spelling & Phonics

Grades 4–5

Writer
Carol Besanko

Editorial Director
Susan A. Blair

Project Manager
Erica L. Varney

Cover Designer
Roman Laszok

Interior Designer
Mark Sayer

Production Editor
Maggie Jones

SGS-SFI/COC-US09/5501

The classroom teacher may reproduce materials in this book for classroom use only.
The reproduction of any part for an entire school or school system is strictly prohibited.
No part of this publication may be transmitted, stored, or recorded in any form
without written permission from the publisher.

1   2   3   4   5   6   7   8   9   10
ISBN 0-8251-4777-8
Copyright © 2004
Walch Publishing
P. O. Box 658 • Portland, Maine 04104-0658
walch.com
Printed in the United States of America

Table of Contents

To the Teacher v

Consonants 1–36
- Initial Consonants 1
- Middle Consonants 4
- Final Consonants 5
- Hard and Soft "C" and "G" 6
- Consonant Digraphs 12
- Final Consonants "F," "L," and "S" 25
- Final Consonants 27
- Consonant Blends 28
- Silent Consonants 34

Vowels 37–51
- Short Vowels 37
- Short Vowel Sounds "AM" and "AN" 46
- Short Vowel Rulebreakers 48
- Schwa 50

Syllabication 52–81
- Long Vowels/Open Syllables 52
- Silent "E" 57
- Closed Syllables 63
- Closed Syllables and Silent "E" 69
- Open and Closed Syllables 74
- Words with Two Open Syllables 77
- Open Syllables and Silent "E" 79
- "LE" Syllable 80

Plurals 82–91
- "S" and "ES" 82
- Changing "Y" to "I" 87
- Words That End in "O" 88
- Changing "F" to "V" 89
- Irregular Plurals 90
- Review 91

Endings 92–108
- "ING" 92
- "ED" 96
- "ER" 102
- "EST" 106

Daily Skill-Builders

Spelling & Phonics

Grades 4–5

Prefixes 109–113
"UN" and "DIS" 109
"PRE" and "RE" 110
"MIS" and "NON" 111
"OVER" and "IM" 112
Review 113

Suffixes 114–125
"LESS" and "FUL" 114
"Y" and "LY" 117
"TION" and "SION" 119
"ANCE" and "ENCE" 123
Review 125

R-Controlled Vowels 126–134

Vowel Digraphs 135–159
"AY," "AI," and "EI" 135
"EE," "EY," and "EA" 140
"IE" and "EI" 147
"OA," "OE," and "OW" 149
"OU" 154
"AW" and "AU" 157

Diphthongs 160–162

Copycat Sounds 163–164
"IGH" 163
"EIGH" 164

Compound Words 165–166

Contractions 167–171

Possessives 172–173

Vocabulary 174–178
Antonyms 174
Synonyms 175
Homophones 176
Homographs 177
Multiple Meanings 178

Review 179–180

Answer Key 181

To the Teacher

Introduction to *Daily Skill-Builders*

The *Daily Skill-Builders* series began as an expansion of our popular *Daily Warm-Ups* series for grades 5–adult. Word spread, and eventually elementary teachers were asking for something similar. Just as *Daily Warm-Ups* do, *Daily Skill-Builders* turn extra classroom minutes into valuable learning time. Not only do these activities reinforce necessary skills for elementary students, they also make skill-drilling an engaging and informative process. Each book in this series contains 180 reproducible activities—one for each day of the school year!

How to Use *Daily Skill-Builders*

Daily Skill-Builders are easy to use—simply photocopy the day's activity and distribute it. Each page is designed to take approximately ten to fifteen minutes. Many teachers choose to use them in the morning when students are arriving at school or in the afternoon before students leave for the day. They are also a great way to switch gears from one subject to another. No matter how you choose to use them, extra classroom minutes will never go unused again.

Building Skills for All Students

The *Daily Skill-Builders* activities give you great flexibility. The activities can be used effectively in a variety of ways to help all your students develop important skills, regardless of their level.

Depending on the needs of your students and your curriculum goals, you may want the entire class to do the same skill-builder, or you may select specific activities for different students. There are several activities for each topic covered in *Daily Skill-Builders*, so you

can decide which and how many activities to use to help students to master a particular skill.

If a student does not complete an activity in the allotted time, he or she may complete it as homework, or you may allow more time the next day to finish. If a student completes a skill-builder early, you may want to assign another. *Daily Skill-Builders* give you options that work for you.

Students in one grade level vary in their abilities, so each *Daily Skill-Builders* covers two grades. In a fourth-grade class, for example, some students may need the books for grades 3–4. Other students may need the greater challenge presented in the 4–5 books. Since all the books look virtually the same and many of the activities are similar, the students need not know that they are working at different levels.

No matter how you choose to use them, *Daily Skill-Builders* will enhance your teaching. They are easy for you to use, and your students will approach them positively as they practice needed skills.

Name _____

Consonant Countdown

There are 26 letters of the alphabet. Twenty-one of them are consonants. **Consonants** are letters that are not vowels.

> **Vowels** are **a, e, i, o, u.**
> **Rulebreaker:** The letter **y** can be a consonant or a vowel.

1. Write the consonants on the following lines, including the letter **y**:

   __ __ __ __ __ __ __ __ __ __ __
   __ __ __ __ __ __ __ __ __ __

Write the beginning consonant sound you hear on the line next to each picture.

2.	3.	4.
5.	6.	7.
8.	9.	10.

Initial Consonants

Daily Skill-Builders Spelling & Phonics 4–5
walch.com © 2004 Walch Publishing

1

Name _____

A Box Filled with Consonants

Use consonants from each box to complete the words below.

1. | b c d
     f g |

2. | j k l
     m n |

3. | r s t
     v w |

4. | h p q(u)
     y z |

___entist   ___oke   ___ust   ___oo

___lag   ___om   ___ideo   ___ellow

___reen   ___adder   ___nake   ___appy

___aby   ___ing   ___itch   ___izza

___abin   ___umber   ___eeth   ___een

Notice the letter **q** does not act alone. The letter **q** is usually followed by the letter **u**. Qu often sounds like /kw/.

5. Write **qu** on the lines to complete these words. Then read each word.

   ___ack   ___iet   ___ite   ___ick   ___iz

6. What do you call the letters of the alphabet that are not vowels?

   _____

Name _____

Missing Consonants

Write the missing consonant on the line to complete the word in each sentence below.

1. Sam's dog will not ___ite.

2. The water will ___rip off the roof.

3. The baby will ___ry when she's hungry.

4. Will you ___elp me clean the house?

5. Sometimes, there is a ___ainbow after a storm.

6. I like to eat ___opcorn when I watch ___ovies.

7. Ben likes to walk on the ___rail.

8. Steve will ___ax his car to keep it bright and shiny.

9. Beth's favorite color is ___ellow.

10. When it's ___ero degrees outside, it's cold!

Initial Consonants

Daily Skill-Builders Spelling & Phonics 4–5
walch.com © 2004 Walch Publishing

3

Name _____

Stuck in the Middle

Write the correct consonant on the line to complete each word below.

1. | k t |
   |------|
   | toas__er |
   | bas__et |

2. | b p |
   |------|
   | ap__le |
   | base__all |

3. | c r |
   |------|
   | hair__ut |
   | wo__ld |

4. | h z |
   |------|
   | zig__ag |
   | up__ill |

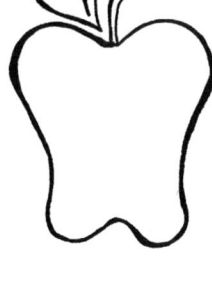

5. | f j |
   |------|
   | pa__amas |
   | fire__ly |

6. | g k |
   |------|
   | than__ful |
   | for__ot |

7. | s v |
   |------|
   | mu__ic |
   | pre__iew |

8. | w n |
   |------|
   | wrist__atch |
   | ken__el |

9. | m l |
   |------|
   | val__ey |
   | wind__ill |

10. | d x |
    |------|
    | tu__edo |
    | win__ow |

Daily Skill-Builders Spelling & Phonics 4–5
walch.com © 2004 Walch Publishing

Middle Consonants

Name _____

In the End

Many words end with a consonant. Some words end in the letters **h, w,** and **y,** but these letters do not make the consonant sounds heard at the beginning or the middle of words. English words do not end in the letters **j, v,** and **q.**

Write the correct consonant on the line to complete each word below.

1. **b c d f g**
   - preten___
   - stif___
   - bi___
   - picni___
   - cobwe___

2. **k l m n p**
   - ho___
   - tas___
   - albu___
   - cabi___
   - bal___

3. **r s t x z**
   - buz___
   - tu___
   - regre___
   - dres___
   - docto___

Write the letter that completes the word.

4.
   lea ___

5.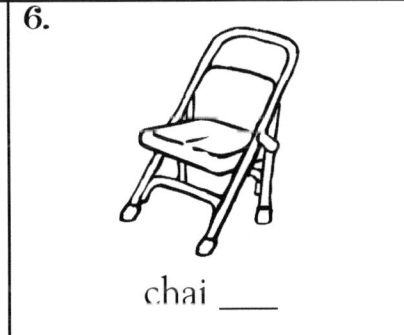
   came ___

6. chai ___

Write words of your own that end in the following consonants:

7. _____ b   8. _____ m   9. _____ r

_____ d   _____ n   _____ t

_____ g   _____ p   _____ x

Final Consonants

Hard and Soft "C"

When the consonant **c** is followed by the vowels **e, i,** or **y,** the **c** sounds soft like the letter **s.**

Examples: nice /nīs¢/   city /sĭt ē/   icy /ī sē/

When **c** is followed by any other letter, it sounds hard like the letter **k.**

Examples: cat /kăt/   cake /kāk¢/

Read the sentences below. Write **hard** or **soft** on the line to tell what the underlined **c** stands for.

1. I just went on the ride twi<u>c</u>e in a row! _____

2. What is the pri<u>c</u>e of that pair of pants? _____

3. Do you want to enter the singing <u>c</u>ontest with me? _____

4. Who won the ra<u>c</u>e yesterday? _____

5. My pen<u>c</u>il is not in my desk where I left it. _____

6. Make a wish and blow out the <u>c</u>andles on your cake. _____

7. Be sure to thank Grandma for the money in your birthday <u>c</u>ard. _____

8. My parents bought me a silver bra<u>c</u>elet for my birthday. _____

9. My favorite candy is the one with the caramel in the <u>c</u>enter. _____

10. I hope they <u>c</u>ancel school because of the snow. _____

Name _____

Hard and Soft "G"

When the consonant **g** is followed by the vowels **e, i,** or **y**, the g usually has a soft sound like the letter **j**.

Examples: age /āj/   gym /jĭm/

When **g** is followed by any other letter, it usually has a hard sound like the letter **g**.

Examples: game /gām/   gold /gōld/

Read the words in the box below. If the word has a soft **g**, write it in the **Soft G** column. If the word has a hard **g**, write it in the **Hard G** column.

| page | magic | dragon | gentle | huge | legend |
| garlic | goose | giant | goat | digest | going |

Soft G   Hard G

_____   _____
_____   _____
_____   _____
_____   _____
_____   _____
_____   _____

Hard and Soft g

Name _____

Sounding Hard and Soft

When the letters **c** and **g** are followed by the vowels **e, i,** or **y**, the **c** has a soft sound /s/, and the **g** has a soft sound /j/. If **c** and **g** are not followed by these vowels, **c** makes the sound of /k/, and **g** makes the sound of /g/.

Examples: cent   giant

Write the sound the **c** or **g** makes in each word.

1. wagon /___/
2. celery /___/
3. cotton /___/
4. orange /___/
5. angel /___/
6. juice /___/
7. cereal /___/
8. garden /___/
9. recess /___/
10. picture /___/
11. gentle /___/
12. game /___/

Use only the words from above with soft **c** and **g** to complete the sentences below.

13. I like to eat _____ with peanut butter or cream cheese.

14. For Halloween last year I was a beautiful _____.

15. Will you peel my _____ for me?

16. I eat a bowl of _____ every morning for breakfast.

17. We couldn't go outside for _____ today because it was raining.

18. Please be very _____ with the baby so you don't wake her up.

Name _____

Picturing Hard and Soft Sounds

Write the name of the picture on the lines provided. Then write the sound the **c** or **g** makes in each word.

1. _ _ _ /_/	2. _ _ _ _ /_/	3. _ _ _ _ _ /_/
4. _ _ _ _ _ /_/	5. _ _ _ _ _ _ /_/	6. _ _ _ /_/
7. _ _ _ _ _ _ _ /_/	8. _ _ _ /_/	9. _ _ _ _ _ _ /_/
10. _ _ _ _ _ _ /_/	11. _ _ _ _ _ _ /_/	12. _ _ _ _ /_/

Hard and Soft c and g

Name _____

Hard or Soft?

Remember: The **c** has the soft sound /s/ and the **g** has the soft sound /j/ when they are followed by the vowels **e, i,** or **y.** When **c** and **g** are followed by other letters, they have the hard sounds: **c** /k/, **g** /g/.

> The letter **c** has two sounds: /k/ or /s/
> The letter **g** has two sounds: /g/ or /j/

Write the sound **c** or **g** makes on the line next to each word.

1. care /___/
2. garlic /___/, /___/
3. city /___/
4. gentle /___/
5. Cathy /___/
6. game /___/
7. Cindy /___/
8. going /___/
9. candy /___/
10. gem /___/
11. decide /___/
12. magic /___/, /___/
13. pencil /___/
14. chug /___/
15. declare /___/
16. migrate /___/
17. replace /___/
18. agent /___/
19. pancake /___/
20. bagpipe /___/

Name _____

Puzzling "C" and "G"

Complete the crossword puzzle using words with hard and soft **c** and **g** from the box. Once you write each word in the puzzle, write the sound **c** (/k/ or /s/) or **g** (/g/ or /j/) makes in the space after each clue.

cabin
calf
center
cotton
dragon
excited
face
garden
geese
giraffe
large
stage

Across
2. an animal with a long neck /__/
4. big /__/
7. looking forward to something /__/
10. small house /__/
11. middle of something /__/

Down
1. baby cow /__/
2. plural of goose /__/
3. where your eyes, nose, and mouth are /__/
5. where vegetables grow /__/
6. where performances take place /__/
8. clothes are made from this /__/
9. fire-breathing creature /__/

Hard and Soft c and g

Name _____

Two Consonants—One Sound

Consonant digraphs are two consonants together in a certain order that make one sound.

Examples: **sh** as in *ship*, **ch** as in *chip*, **th** as in *thin*, **wh** as in *whip*, **ck** as in *stick*

> **Rules to know:**
> Words do not begin with **ck**.
> Words do not end with **wh**.

Circle all the digraphs in the words below.

1.	ship	chip	thin	when	stick
2.	shop	chin	then	whip	stack
3.	shed	chop	this	whistle	sick
4.	wish	much	bath	where	tuck
5.	mash	such	moth	white	clock

Write the digraphs on the lines below, and give a one-word example of each.

6. ____ _____

7. ____ _____

8. ____ _____

9. ____ _____

10. ____ _____

Name _____

Quick Digraph Review

Even though it usually has two sounds /kw/, **qu** is like a digraph. **Remember:** Digraphs are two letters together that make one sound. Think of **qu** as a digraph because the letters go together to make a pair. The letter **q** does not work without the letter **u**.

Here are some **qu** words with the /kw/ sound:

queen   **qu**ick   **qu**it   **qu**iz   **qu**ack

Digraph sounds:
qu /kw/   sh /sh/   ch /ch/   wh /hw/   th /th/   ck /ck/

Write the sound of each digraph on the line. Then write a word for each digraph.

1. qu   /__/   _____
2. sh   /__/   _____
3. ch   /__/   _____
4. wh   /__/   _____
5. th   /__/   _____
6. ck   /__/   _____

Write digraphs on the lines to make words. There may be more than one choice.

7. ___ot   ___ick   ___ip   ma___
8. ___op   ___ut   ___at   su___
9. ___ack   ___en   ___ed   wi___
10. ___ite   ___in   ___ere   sta___
11. ___is   ___an   ___iz   clo___
12. ___ose   ___ese   ___urch wat___

Consonant Digraphs *qu, sh, ch, wh, th,* and *ck*

Daily Skill-Builders Spelling & Phonics 4–5
walch.com © 2004 Walch Publishing

13

Name _____

Digraph Search

In the word search, circle the words with the consonant digraphs **ch, sh, th, wh,** and **ck**. Words can be found vertically, horizontally, diagonally, or backwards. *Hint:* There are 18 words!

```
E K I F C D L Y N H I D P X
G D E T T C S M Y N K U B Y
M Z H U L H I Q H P I H C P
W L H Z S O C C W F I N G D
Y S G H F P K X X D W P F W
P W I C T H A T Q U Q M N V
J P H L W H I C H C D E H G
D I O O D D R H N K H V H D
E P M C N D T U I T S I S L
M L A K E I K I H O Y P I S
Q Z Q H W V M Q C A E J N I
K X S E F W Y K T S H R I H
Z E T I H W S M O O T H F S
I T F N H D E D L M B Y D P
```

Daily Skill-Builders Spelling & Phonics 4–5
walch.com © 2004 Walch Publishing

Consonant Digraphs *ch, sh, wh, th,* and *ck*

14

Name _____

"Ph" or "F"?

The consonant digraph **ph** makes the /f/ sound. **Remember:** A consonant digraph has two consonants that together make one sound.

Example: phone /fōn/.

Each word below contains the /f/ sound. Say the word. If the word is misspelled, spell it correctly on the line. If the word is already spelled correctly, write **correct** on the line.

1. foto _____      2. trophy _____

3. traphic _____      4. dolfin _____

5. phog _____      6. elephant _____

7. graff _____      8. alfabet _____

9. gofer _____      10. golph _____

11. orfan _____   12. phonics _____

Consonant Digraph *ph*

One Sound—Two Spellings

To make the /ch/ sound at the end of a word, **tch** is used only when the sound comes after a short vowel.

Examples: witch 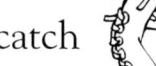   catch

To make the /ch/ sound at the end of a word with two vowels (a long vowel sound), use **ch**.

Examples: beach   peach

To make the /ch/ sound at the end of a word that has a consonant between the short vowel and the /ch/ sound, use **ch**.

Examples: bench   lunch

Each word below contains the /ch/ sound. Say the word. If the word is misspelled, spell it correctly on the line. If the word is spelled correctly, write **correct** on the line. Use the rules above to help you.

1. ich _____
2. skech _____
3. teatcher _____
4. puntch _____
5. kichen _____
6. swich _____
7. reatch _____
8. munch _____
9. pich _____
10. batch _____

Name _____

"PH" and "TCH"

On the line, write the word that names each picture.

1. 　2. 　3. 　4.

_____ _____ _____ _____

Fill in each line with the word from the box that best completes the sentence.

ketchup	kitchen	catch	switch
scratch	witch	ditch	stretch

5. Brad reached his glove out to _____ a baseball.

6. Sally likes _____ on her French fries.

7. The cat loves it when I _____ its chin.

8. For Halloween, Rosa will dress up as a _____.

9. In gym class, we always _____ before we run.

10. Please eat your lunch at the table in the _____.

11. The car skidded on the icy road and rolled into the _____.

12. Will you _____ sides with me?

Consonant Digraphs *ph* and *tch*

Name _____

Searching for Digraphs

In the word search, circle only words from the box that have the /ch/ or /f/ sound. Words can be found vertically, horizontally, diagonally, or backwards.

hash	pitch	clock	graph	photo
catch	street	phonics	cinder	parcel
ketchup	dolphin	stretch	tricky	trophy

```
S W T V U B Y A S N L O P D
R E Q W R L Y N H P T S L W
T L M Y M H I K O Y H X S E
E U Z N P H S C I N O H P Y
P W L O P V S Q X X J S X B
Z E R L R O K T Y Y G M P H
L T O N A S T K R E U Q I G
N D Y R T H E O G E P F T D
D U J R P T C W H L T A C J
R K A A C I A T K P W C H U
T N R H W Z T K C W A I H L
Y G U T F O C J W D D B Y Z
M P X C I V H L H S S R Z Q
O U G B S R Q M L H B G I O
```

Daily Skill-Builders Spelling & Phonics 4–5
walch.com © 2004 Walch Publishing

Consonant Digraphs *ph* and *tch*

Name _____

Two Sounds of "CH"

The letters **ch** have two sounds. In most words, they sound like /ch/ as in the word *chip*. The letters **ch** can also sound like /k/ as in the word *ache*.

Read the words. Then circle the letters that signal the /k/ sound in each word.

1. school   Chris   ache   stomach   chemical

2. echo   chorus   chord   anchor   character

Match the words with the definitions below. Write the letter of the correct definition on the line.

_____ 3. school   **a.** a heavy hook used to keep boats from drifting

_____ 4. echo   **b.** a place where people go to learn

_____ 5. stomach   **c.** a repeating sound

_____ 6. chorus   **d.** the abdomen or belly

_____ 7. anchor   **e.** a group of singers

_____ 8. chord   **f.** a person in a play or a book

_____ 9. chemical   **g.** a combination of musical sounds

_____ 10. character   **h.** a substance used in chemistry, drugs, and medicine

Write your own sentences using the following words.

11. anchor _____

12. chorus _____

Consonant Digraph *ch*

Name _____

A "CK" Picnic

The digraph **ck** has a /k/ sound. **Note:** Words such as *clock, stick, lack, truck,* and *deck* have only one syllable, and they all end with **ck**. When making the /k/ sound at the end of words with more than one syllable, the sound is still /k/, but the spelling is often only with a **c** and not with the digraph **ck**.

Examples: pi**c**nic   top**ic**

Note: There is no **ck** spelling at the end of the words, but the sound you hear is still /k/.

1. Write these ocean words in alphabetical order and say the sounds.

   Pacific   Atlantic   Arctic
   _____   _____   _____

Match the words with the definitions below. Write the letter of the correct definition on the line.

2. _____ public   a. subject

3. _____ panic   b. eating food outside

4. _____ picnic   c. a state of being scared

5. _____ topic   d. the people as a whole

6. Write the spelling of the /k/ sound to complete each two-syllable word.

   comi___   septi___   rusti___   graphi___

"CK" in the Middle

The digraph **ck** /k/ often comes in the middle of a word.

Read the words and match them with the pictures. Write the correct letter on the line. Also, circle the **ck** in each word.

1. jacket ____
2. pocket ____
3. locket ____
4. cricket ____
5. packet ____
6. ticket ____
7. rocket ____
8. racket ____

a.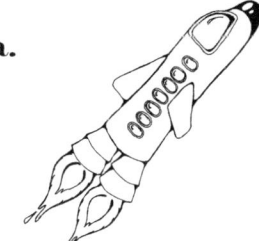

b.

c.

d.

e.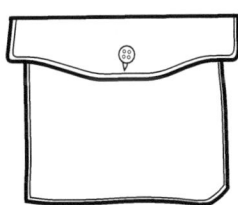

f.

g.

h.

Name _____

What's at the End?

The consonant digraphs **ng** and **nk** are often used at the ends of words.

Circle the **ng** and **nk** words below that are correct.

1. dunk   crang   stronk   bring   wing
2. thank   plang   swink   chunk   wronk
3. blang   string   pronk   flink   sang
4. lung   lunk   link   plunk   long

Write **ng** or **nk** on the line to correctly complete each word.

5. ki____   dri____   sku____   dri____   tha____
6. stro____   swi____   tru____   ju____   wro____
7. stri____   ba____   spa____   ho____   lo____

Write your own sentences using the words listed below.

8. thank _____
   _____

9. bring _____
   _____

10. strong _____
    _____

Final Consonant Digraphs *ng* and *nk*

Name _____

Picture This!

Write the name of the picture on the lines.

Now, fill in each line with the word from the box that best completes the sentence.

| pink | sang | hang | bunk |
| bank | ring | sink | think |

7. I love your new diamond _____.

8. We stopped at the _____ to get some money.

9. The twins sleep on _____ beds.

10. We can _____ that picture over the kitchen _____.

11. I don't _____ you should wear that _____ shirt.

12. My sister _____ my favorite song.

Final Consonant Digraphs *ng* and *nk*

Name _____

"NG" or "NK"?

Fill in each line with the word from the box that best completes the sentence.

| ping-pong | honk | sank | ring | sang | thank |
| strong | sink | bunk | song | stung | hang |

1. Ed likes to play _____ with Pedro.

2. The ship _____ to the bottom of the ocean.

3. My older sister sleeps on the top _____.

4. I am so _____ I can carry you on my back.

5. Liz _____ a duet with Taylor in the talent show.

6. I love the _____ playing on the radio.

7. That bee just _____ me on the arm.

8. Please _____ the painting on the wall.

9. I will _____ Mom for the new, shiny bike she gave me.

10. Please put the dirty dish in the _____.

11. _____ your horn if you pass me walking down the street.

12. I dropped my _____ down the drain, but the plumber found it!

Daily Skill-Builders Spelling & Phonics 4–5
walch.com © 2004 Walch Publishing

Final Consonant Digraphs *ng* and *nk*

Name _____

A Final Letter

When the letters **f, l,** and **s** follow a short vowel sound, the letters are usually doubled—in other words, they get a bonus letter.

   Examples: stuff   bell   miss

Add the correct double consonants (**ff, ll,** or **ss**) to complete the words below.

1. dre____   do____   me____   she____

2. o____   che____   se____   stu____

Read the sentences below. Circle the words that are missing a bonus letter at the end. Write the correct word(s) on the lines. Some words with bonus letters may be spelled correctly.

3. Wil you help me move this stuf off the window sil? _____

4. Your room is stil a mes. _____

5. We always huf and puff when we climb the hil. _____

6. Please pas me that bucket of shels. _____

7. Can I buy a new dress for my dol? _____

8. Mis Bell, wil you play ches with me? _____

Here's a Rulebreaker: The sound of **all** is /ôl/.

   Example: ball

9. List as many **all** words as you can think of below.

_____

Final Consonants *f, l,* and *s*

Name _____

Add a Letter

Read the sentences below, and circle all the words with bonus letters.
Remember: The bonus letters are **f, l,** and **s.**

Examples: stiff   shell   fuss

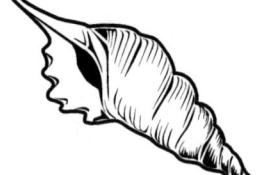

1. The bell will ring at 8:00 A.M.

2. My teacher's name is Miss Bess.

3. The girls will shop at the big mall.

4. There is moss on the north side of that tall tree.

5. Bill will sell his chess set at the mall.

6. Stay off the hill so you don't fall.

7. Please toss the ball to the child with the doll.

8. Jill's dress was a big mess.

Write four sentences using bonus-letter words of your choice.

9. _____

10. _____

11. _____

12. _____

Daily Skill-Builders Spelling & Phonics 4–5
walch.com © 2004 Walch Publishing

Final Consonants *f, l,* and *s*

Name _____

Sounds in a Name

Remember: Consonant digraphs have one sound—**sh, ch, ck, th, wh**.

Each digraph needs to be written together on one line.
   Example: Chuck = **Ch** u **ck**
Bonus letters need to stay together on one line (**ff, ll, ss**).
   Example: Will = W i **ll**

Write each sound in the names below on a separate line.

1. Tom	= ___ ___ ___	2. Tim	= ___ ___ ___
3. Bob	= ___ ___ ___	4. Bill	= ___ ___ ___
5. Chet	= ___ ___ ___	6. Josh	= ___ ___ ___
7. Rob	= ___ ___ ___	8. Beth	= ___ ___ ___
9. Jeff	= ___ ___ ___	10. Jill	= ___ ___ ___
11. Chad	= ___ ___ ___	12. Ted	= ___ ___ ___
13. Deb	= ___ ___ ___	14. Jack	= ___ ___ ___
15. Kim	= ___ ___ ___	16. Liz	= ___ ___ ___
17. Nick	= ___ ___ ___	18. Rich	= ___ ___ ___
19. Ross	= ___ ___ ___	20. Bev	= ___ ___ ___
21. Ben	= ___ ___ ___	22. Ken	= ___ ___ ___
23. Jed	= ___ ___ ___	24. Pat	= ___ ___ ___
25. Roz	= ___ ___ ___	26. Don	= ___ ___ ___
27. Peg	= ___ ___ ___	28. Rick	= ___ ___ ___
29. Seth	= ___ ___ ___	30. Meg	= ___ ___ ___
31. Jud	= ___ ___ ___	32. Bess	= ___ ___ ___
33. Kris	= ___ ___ ___ ___	34. Cliff	= ___ ___ ___

Consonant Digraphs and Final Consonants

Name _____

Blend Together

Consonant blends are consonants that are together and keep their own sounds. A blend can be at the beginning, middle, or end of a word.

Examples: brag   poster   milk

Here is a list of blends found in many words:

bl	dr	gr	sk	st	scr	ft	lt
br	fl	pl	sl	sw	spl	mp	ld
cr	fr	pr	sn	tr	str	lk	lp
cl	gl	sc	sp	tw	ct	lf	nd

Use the blends in the triangles to make words. Use each blend only once.

1.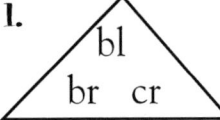

___ue

___ick

___y

2.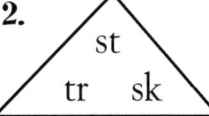

___ing

___in

___ue

3.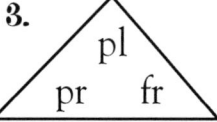

___ate

___ice

___og

4.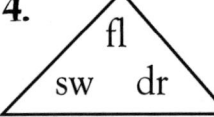

___ink

___ock

___im

5.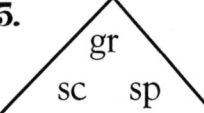

___een

___ine

___ar

6.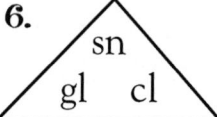

___ake

___ad

___ock

28 *Daily Skill-Builders* Spelling & Phonics 4–5
walch.com © 2004 Walch Publishing

Consonant Blends

Name _____

Beginning Blends

Write the sounds from each column below to complete the words beginning with blends. Say the word after completing each one.

1. -ing	2. -and	3. -ack	4. -ick	5. -ock
st____	st____	bl____	br____	st____
sl____	br____	st____	st____	fl____
br____	bl____	sn____	fl____	cl____
sw____	gl____	tr____	tr____	bl____
cl____	gr____	sl____	sl____	cr____

Write the blend from each word on the line next to each word below. Say the sound in each blend as you write it.

6. plan ____	7. trick ____	8. cling ____
crack ____	snag ____	swell ____
blue ____	slap ____	spine ____
brave ____	twig ____	flame ____
glad ____	crib ____	score ____

Now write two sentences of your own. Include as many blends from above as you can.

9. _____

10. _____

Consonant Blends

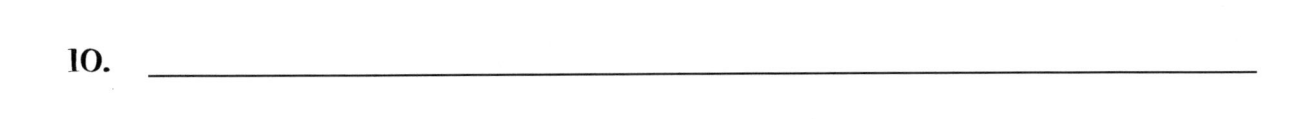

Name _____

Blends, Blends, and More Blends

Sometimes there are three consonants in a row that may be a blend or a digraph-blend. A three-letter blend has three consonants in a row that keep their own sounds, such as **spl**, **scr**, and **spr**. A **digraph-blend** is a digraph combined with another consonant, such as **shr**, **squ**, **nch**, or **lch**.

The chart below shows the sound for each blend or digraph-blend and a word for each.

Blend	Sound	Word	Digraph-blend	Sound	Word
spl	/s p l/	splash	shr	/sh r/	shred
scr	/s c r/	scram	nch	/n ch/	inch
spr	/s p r/	spring	lch	/l ch/	mulch
str	/s t r/	strap	squ	/s qu/	squeak

Circle the three-letter blends and digraph-blends in the following words.

1. scrub	2. string	3. spleen	4. scrape	5. stripe	6. screw
scream	straw	splash	scratch	munch	inch
shrub	shrine	bench	bunch	lunch	stride

Write the correct words from the box in the sentences below.

street	lunch	stream	scribble

7. I will have pizza and milk for _____.

8. Jen will catch fish in the _____.

9. The toddler likes to _____ with her crayons.

10. Look both ways before you cross the _____.

Name _____

Blends at the End

Look at the blend at the end of each word in the box below. Say each word, and listen for the blend. Then use the words to complete the sentences.

blond	fast	shelf	milk
desk	belt	held	jump

1. My sister has _____ hair.

2. How _____ can you run?

3. Please, put the books on the _____.

4. Sam likes to drink _____ at lunchtime.

5. Please sit at your _____ and raise your hand.

6. Grandpa uses a _____ to hold up his pants.

7. The mother _____ the baby in her arms.

8. The kangaroo can _____ high.

Some words have two blends, one at the beginning, and one at the end. Find all the blends in the words below and circle them.

9. blend   craft   brisk   clump   trust

10. crust   frost   clasp   stamp   spend

Consonant Blends

Name

Begin with Blends

In the word search, circle only the words from the box that have beginning blends. Words can be found vertically, horizontally, diagonally, or backwards.

bled	pond	swim	belt	sled	crib	glad
drag	flub	disk	drop	silk	flat	fast
must	plug	crab	frog	trot	jump	slop

```
J F E Q X T B G N K I D S B
W F J B M G N Y G Z M U B I
S D R O P B U L F U I A R C
T P D O B S K T A O R F B N
E G C V G L M Q A C U G L L
R Y U P W E I G Q L Z U E I
Z N R L H D W T F F F F D E
I M P O P Y S B I R C I G O
O H R L F T U N K H S L Y D
P A Y V R P W D J U U L D Q
D C I O O H X A D A X R E P
S J T L R J V L L M A C N S
L D S M Z H S G G G N O Q A
I J D Y E W M P S O G C F P
```

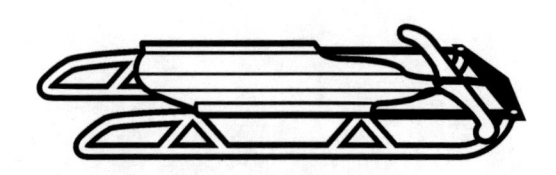

32 Daily Skill-Builders Spelling & Phonics 4–5
walch.com © 2004 Walch Publishing

Consonant Blends

Name _____

Now, End with Blends

In the word search, circle only the words from the box that end with blends. Words can be found vertically, horizontally, diagonally, and backwards.

drop	held	belt	jump	desk	sled
bask	crib	fast	shelf	plug	must
disk	pond	frog	glad	fist	silk

```
T Y H D W M P O F T X S Y B
L F L K S V C F M D S F T I
D T I I Y F M P U A L H S P
S V L S P Y M C S M M Z A H
A K F R T U N E T V Q P F K
T K I Y J O B E F X Y H C F
U M N U D F D A I Y K K T E
K S H E L F I T S D E S K C
P Z X C P U S M I K H D G G
I H V F C S K T V E S N E R
L R S Y T R T A L G Z R E Y
D M T F D S R D Q E K N S L
Z N H D N O P S W X B P R O
Y I N E R T G Y Y D Q A O P
```

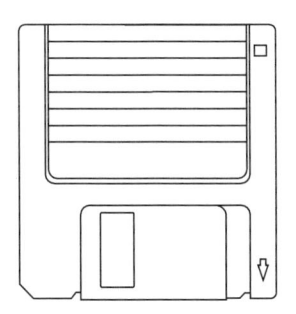

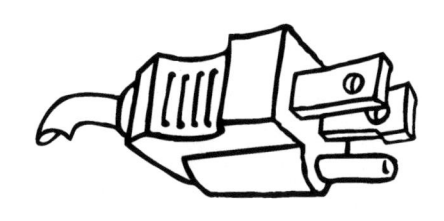

Consonant Blends

Daily Skill-Builders Spelling & Phonics 4–5
walch.com © 2004 Walch Publishing

Name _____

The "K" Is Silent

The letters **kn** make the **n** /n/ sound, and the **k** is silent. For example, the word *knee* sounds like /nē/. **Note:** The **k** is not heard.

1. Read the following words. Then circle the letters that make the **n** /n/ sound. Cross out the silent letter.

   know   knew   known   knowledge

   knock   knee   kneel   knapsack

   knot   knack   knob   knuckle

   knight   knife   knit   knickknack

Fill in each line with the word from the box that best completes the sentence.

| knapsack | knuckle | knows | knocked | knees | knob |

2. Debbie _____ how to do a high jump.

3. Tony hurt his _____ when he _____ on the door.

4. Your _____ must be strong to run fast.

5. Lauren's _____ is filled with notebooks.

6. Please turn the _____ slowly when opening the door.

Name _____

That Quiet "W"!

The letters **wr** make the **r** /r/ sound, and the **w** is silent. For example, the word *write* sounds like /rīt/. **Note:** The **w** is not heard.

1. Read the following words. Then circle the letters that make the **r** /r/ sound. Cross out the silent letter.

   write   wrote   written   wrist

   wrap   wreath   wrong   wrinkle

   wrestle   wreck   wrecker   wristband

Fill in each line with the word from the box that best completes the sentence.

wrote	wrong	wreath	wrap	wrinkle
write	wrist	written	wreck	

2. Please _____ your name on the top line.

3. It is _____ to cheat.

4. Jamie had _____ three pages in her notebook.

5. There is a _____ in Joanie's dress.

6. The bad _____ destroyed the car.

7. Tammy broke her _____ when she fell to the ground.

8. Please _____ the birthday gifts.

9. Jackie _____ a letter to the editor.

10. We hang a _____ on our door during the holidays.

Silent Consonant *w*

Name _____

Silent "B"

The letters **mb** usually stand for **m** as in *climb*. The **b** is silent.

Look at the pictures below. Circle yes if the name of the picture has the letters **mb** in it. Circle no if it does not.

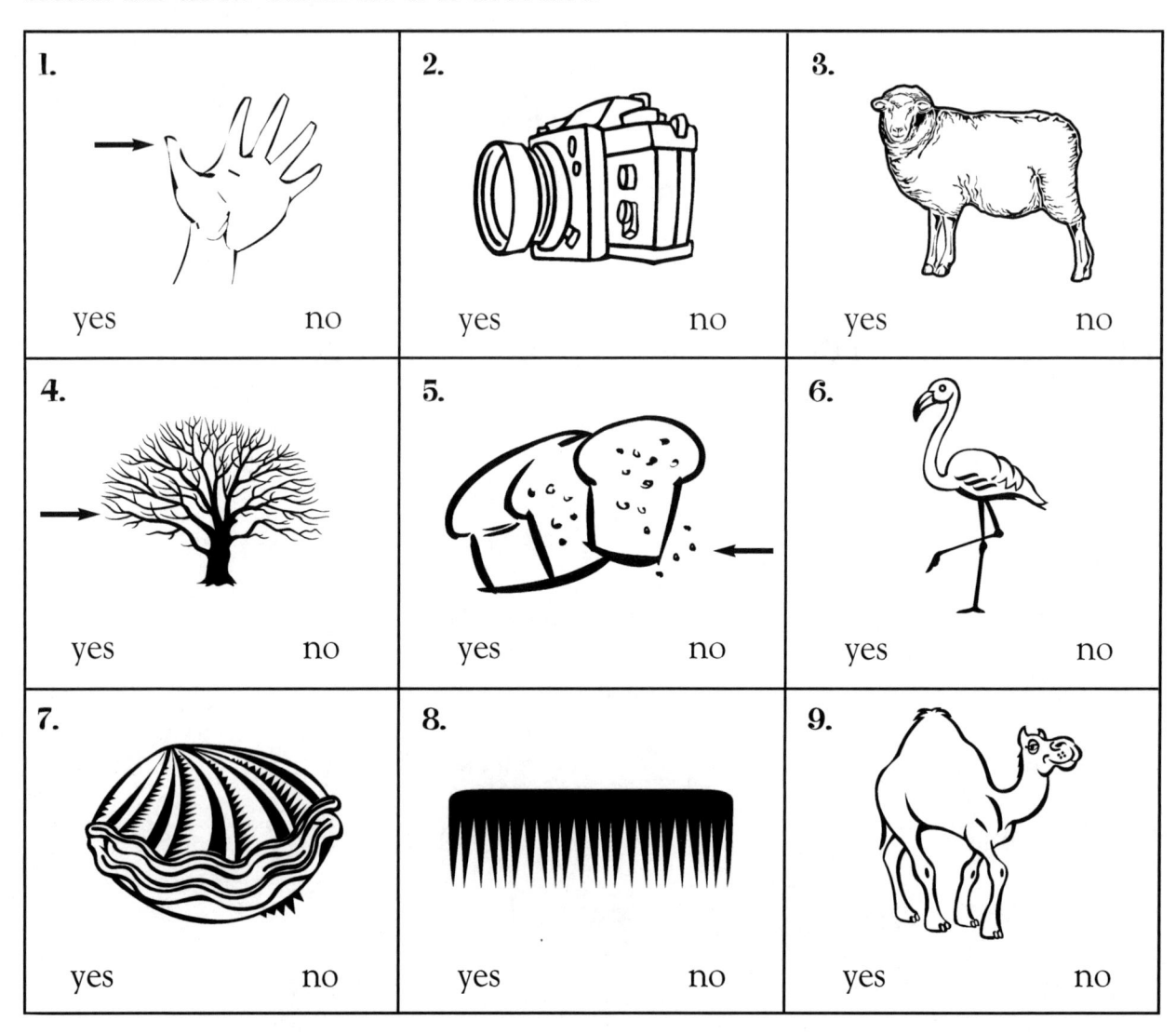

1. yes no	2. yes no	3. yes no
4. yes no	5. yes no	6. yes no
7. yes no	8. yes no	9. yes no

Now use two of the picture names from above in sentences of your own.

10. _____

11. _____

Name _____

A Simple Pattern

Short vowel sounds are usually found in a simple pattern—for example, **consonant-vowel-consonant** (CVC) or **vowel-consonant** (VC). Sometimes the consonant can represent more than one consonant, such as a blend or a digraph.

Examples of the **CVC** or **VC** pattern:

CVC	VC
cat dog brag fill wish	if in is

Note: All of the vowels are closed in by one or more consonants, and there are no other vowels in the word.

Here are key words to know when learning short vowel sounds.

apple /ă/   Ed /ĕ/   inch /ĭ/   on /ŏ/   up /ŭ/

Use the following symbol to mark a short vowel sound: ⌣

On each line, write the short vowel sound and mark it short.

1. bag /___/   kit /___/   pet /___/   ill /___/   sack /___/
2. bed /___/   cut /___/   fox /___/   got /___/   chip /___/
3. yell /___/   pop /___/   bug /___/   off /___/   jump /___/
4. mud /___/   in /___/   wed /___/   den /___/   shock /___/
5. What type of vowel do you hear in CVC or VC patterns? _____
6. Write the mark to use when showing a short vowel sound. _____

Short Vowels

Name _____

Picturing Short Vowels

All five vowels have both short and long sounds. These are the sounds of the short vowels:

> Short **a** says /ă/ as in *apple*.
> Short **e** says /ĕ/ as in *Ed*.
> Short **i** says /ĭ/ as in *inch*.
> Short **o** says /ŏ/ as in *on*.
> Short **u** says /ŭ/ as in *up*.

Circle the letter of the short vowel in the name of each picture below.

1. a e / i o u	2. a e / i o u	3. a e / i o u
4. a e / i o u	5. a e / i o u	6. a e / i o u
7. a e / i o u	8. a e / i o u	9. a e / i o u

38 Daily Skill-Builders Spelling & Phonics 4–5
walch.com © 2004 Walch Publishing

Short Vowels

Name _____

They're All Short

Fill in each line with the short-vowel word from the box that best completes the sentence. Mark the short vowels in the words you write on the lines.

snack	math	bed	bell	quick
chip	drop	spot	shut	gum

1. We are not allowed to chew _____ in school.

2. At 8:30 P.M. you have to brush your teeth and get in _____.

3. Don't eat too much for a _____ or you won't be able to finish your dinner.

4. There is a _____ on the rug where I spilled my juice.

5. Come in from recess when you hear the _____.

6. My favorite ice cream flavors are mint chocolate ____ _____ and cookies and cream.

7. You aren't allowed to go out and play until you finish your _____ homework.

8. Please _____ the door behind you so the dog doesn't get outside.

9. Carry this bowl to the table, and please don't _____ it.

10. You have to be _____ because we don't have much time.

Short Vowels

Name _____

A Missing Vowel

On each line, write the correct vowel from the box to make a word.

1. a e b ___ sk	2. a i d ___ sk	3. e i h ___ ld	4. e u b ___ lt
5. o u bl ___ nd	6. i u cr ___ st	7. o a g ___ lf	8. i e ___ lf
9. u o b ___ lk	10. u e w ___ ld	11. i a d ___ sk	12. a i m ___ sk
13. i a bl ___ st	14. a u j ___ mp	15. e i sh ___ lf	16. e u b ___ mp

17. Now write the vowels. _____

Short Vowels

Name_____

Short "A," Short "I"

Write the vowel **a** or **i** on the lines to complete the words in the sentences below.

1. J____m w____ll take Sam to the ball game.

2. We w____ll sw____m in that lake.

3. My c____t can run very f____st.

4. The small sh____p is near the dock.

5. D____d can f____x the broken window.

6. The tall gr____ss needs a tr____m.

7. Br____d w____ll cut down the tree.

8. Mom likes to wear a c____p in the hot sun.

Write the words from above that have the short vowel **a** or **i** on the lines below. Do not write the same word more than once.

9. **Short Vowel a Words**

_____

_____

_____

_____

_____

_____

10. **Short Vowel i Words**

_____

_____

_____

_____

_____

_____

Short Vowels *a* and *i*

Name _____

Short "O," Short "U"

Write the vowel **o** or **u** on the lines to complete the words in the sentences below.

1. B____b did n____t get the big j____b done.

2. Do n____t st____b your toes on the t____b.

3. The p____p was l____st in the thick f____g.

4. There is a black sp____t on the red r____g.

5. Please, l____ck the back door at d____sk.

6. T____m likes to catch small b____gs.

7. We m____st n____t feed the wild f____x.

8. That fr____g can j____mp really high.

Write the words from above that have the short vowel **o** or **u** on the lines below. Do not write the same word more than once.

9. Short Vowel o Words   **10. Short Vowel u Words**

_____ _____   _____ _____

_____ _____   _____ _____

_____ _____   _____ _____

_____ _____   _____ _____

_____ _____

Name _____

Fill in the Vowels

Choose the correct vowels from the column on the left to make the words to the right. Read the words as you fill in the lines.

1.	a e i o u	f___st f___st
2.	a e i o u	s___ll s___ll
3.	a e i o u	m___ss m___ss m___ss m___ss m___ss
4.	a e i o u	b___g b___g b___g b___g b___g
5.	a e i o u	d___g d___g d___g
6.	a e i o u	c___t c___t c___t
7.	a e i o u	m___d m___d m___d
8.	a e i o u	c___p c___p c___p
9.	a e i o u	f___t f___t
10.	a e i o u	s___ck s___ck s___ck s___ck
11.	a e i o u	r___d r___d r___d
12.	a e i o u	st___ck st___ck st___ck st___ck

a e i o u

Short Vowels

Name

Short Vowel Review

Use the vowels from the boxes to complete the words below.

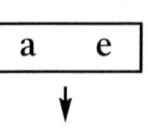

1. | a e |

b____sk
w____ld
st____ff
dr____ss
n____st
cl____sp
st____ck
b____st
h____lp
th____t
sn____p
scr____p
sw____m

2. | i o u |

f____st
b____ss
pl____g
tw____g
fr____st
d____st
shr____mp
cr____sp
wh____ch
b____lk
cr____p
sp____ll
m____lk

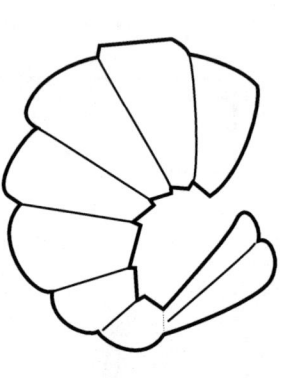

44

Daily Skill-Builders Spelling & Phonics 4–5
walch.com © 2004 Walch Publishing

Short Vowels

Name _____

Rhyme Time

Use lines to connect the rhyming words in each box. **Remember:** Say short vowel sounds while reading the **CVC**-pattern words.

1.
web	fed
red	ten
beg	Deb
men	leg

2.
mob	log
fog	sob
hot	fox
box	got

3.
bat	gap
cap	sad
bag	rag
mad	cat

4.
hid	fit
bit	lid
hip	him
dim	dip

5.
gum	dug
bug	hum
bud	cut
but	mud

6.
belt	fast
blast	pond
blond	crust
bust	felt

7. What type of pattern do the words above follow? _____

Short Vowels

Name

"A" with "M" and "N"

When the vowel **a** is followed by the consonant **m** or **n,** the vowel is considered short. When **am** or **an** is together in this order, the **short a** sounds slightly different from the **a** in *apple*.

Circle the **am** and **an** words that are correct.

1. dam, ham, jam, Pam, ram, Sam, Tam, yam, fram, clam, sham, cram, slam, swam, scram, gram, stam, clamp, cramp, stamp, ramp, camp, hamper, gramper, camper, pamper

2. ban, can, Dan, fan, Jan, man, Nan, pan, pran, ran, tan, van, yan, Stan, clan, than, plan, scan, spran, Fran, stand, bland, brand, crand, land, strand, gland, band, hand, sand, branch, ranch, slant, chant, drant

Write **am** or **an** on the lines to complete the following words.

3. st___d   cr___p   str___d   scr___   cl___p   br___ch

4. ch___t   cl___   h___per   sl___t   b___d   sl___

On the lines, write the words that name the pictures below.

5.	6.	7.	8.
__ a __	__ __ a __	__ a __	__ __ a __ __

Name_____

"AM" or "AN"?

Write **am** or **an** on the lines to complete the words in the sentences below.

1. Max will cook h_____ in a p_____.

2. J_____ got a t_____ at the lake.

3. Leon likes to use a f_____ on a hot day.

4. P_____ r_____ to catch her dog.

5. The kids will ride in a v_____ to the park.

6. S_____ sw_____ faster th_____ D_____.

7. Did you pl_____ to eat all the j_____?

8. T_____ will spend a week at summer c_____p.

Write the **am** and **an** words from above on the lines below.

9.   am

10.   an

Short Vowel Sounds *am* and *an*

Daily Skill-Builders Spelling & Phonics 4–5
walch.com © 2004 Walch Publishing

47

Breaking Rules

When there is one vowel at the beginning or middle of a word, the vowel usually has a short vowel sound.

Examples: a as in căp   e as in bĕd

There are, however, a few rulebreakers. The letter **o** followed by **ld, st,** or **lt** usually stands for the long **o** sound. The letter **i** followed by **ld** and **nd** usually stands for the long **i** sound.

Examples: cōld   mōst   bōlt   wīld   mīnd

There are even rulebreakers to this rulebreaker. Sometimes the **o** and the **i** can still be short when followed by these letters. For example, the **i** in wind (moving air) is short.

Mark the vowels in the words below. Be careful. Some of them may be short.

1. sold   wild   lost   most   hind   molt

2. cost   find   old   kind   behind   mind

Complete each sentence below using one of the words from above.

3. I have the _____ pets of anyone in my class.
4. One of my pets is a bird that was caught in the _____.
5. Sometimes my bird flies up into the attic, and I can't _____ him.
6. My mother hates it when he _____s because there are feathers all over the place.
7. His feathers get all over my room, but I don't _____.
8. We play all _____s of games together.

Name _____

Breaking Rules Again

Fill in each line with the word from the box that best completes the sentence.

| child | kind | hold | find | colt |
| sold | mild | most | told | old |

1. The _____ man is _____ to animals.

2. The _____ likes to gallop on the farm.

3. Greg _____ his baseball cards to Skip.

4. Bev likes _____ salsa with corn chips.

5. The teacher _____ the class to read.

6. Ben has the _____ video games.

7. The puppy cannot _____ the bone.

8. Mom will _____ the sick _____.

Combine the sounds below to make words. Mark the long vowel sound, and read each word as you write it.

9. c + old = _____   10. p + ost = _____

11. w + ild = _____   12. h + ost = _____

13. m + ild = _____   14. v + olt = _____

15. h + ind = _____   16. b + old = _____

Short Vowel Rulebreakers

Name _____

The Schwa

Sometimes any vowel can sound like short **u**. This is called the **schwa** sound. Its symbol looks like an upside-down **e**. It stands for any vowel that is spoken softly. This sound is usually heard in the syllable of a word that is quiet, or unaccented.

Example: camel   /cam əl/

The first syllable, **cam**, is accented. Therefore the **e** sounds like a short **u**.

Circle the letter in each word below that makes the schwa sound.
Remember: The schwa sound makes a short **u** sound.

1. wagon
2. lion
3. seven

4. cabin
5. circus
6. lemon

7. nickel
8. dragon
9. asleep

10. spoken
11. carrot
12. crocodile

Name _____

Searching for Schwa

In the word search below, circle only the words from the box that contain the schwa sound. Words can be found vertically, horizontally, diagonally, and backwards.

golden	alike	nickel	pipe	gossip	music	level
asleep	denim	cotton	barrel	divide	motto	dragon
canal	system	margin	balloon	olive	apron	circus
seven	block	police	salmon	pilot	polite	

```
S B A B Y I S Y S T E M T A L K A F O R
U A D O G S L E D D S A M F K L P E N T
R P W R L P Q N I N S N A P O O J F L B
E R C C X W P V O C K G R J O F T N B L
R O L L A I I S K J P E E V I L O W O S
A N O E B D E N I M I R C X D M I E M P
N C C V H R W R N Y S K W E L S E C I R
J B K E F A B A L L S C H A O B L Z E I
N E D L O G K E L F O M S N S A I E B N
I E W C B O A P I L G R I M W L H J N G
C C V S M N Z O I S C U S H A L E K R T
K N B E L L E L K L B R E A K O C E I I
E E A U F U T I F X O U K W S O C C P M
L F N E S A V T L I S T B U E N H A I E
F I F T E E N E W O F L C G V N T N M M
M A R G I N V S B A E R A M E D L A O O
H L N I S H O T H R I I R D N Z C R M T
E I C H I L L Y E C A N A L V R W Y S T
L K A E C O T T O N C T T S H A D E Z O
V E X L A M P E P A N T S U L E R R A B
```

Schwa

Daily Skill-Builders Spelling & Phonics 4–5
walch.com © 2004 Walch Publishing

51

Name _____

Open and Long

Open syllables have the **consonant-vowel (CV)** pattern. An open syllable ends with a vowel. The vowel is long and says its name. Long vowels are marked with a line.

$$\bar{a} \quad \bar{e} \quad \bar{i} \quad \bar{o} \quad \bar{u}$$

The following words have an open syllable and a long vowel.

Examples: hē   hī   gō

Read the following words and mark the vowels. If the syllable is open, write **O** on the line. If it is not open, write **NO** on the line.

1. no _____
2. bed _____
3. flu _____
4. me _____
5. she _____
6. dog _____
7. kid _____
8. sun _____
9. be _____

If no other vowels are in a syllable, **y** is considered a vowel. When a one-syllable word ends in **y**, it has the long **i** /ī/ sound.

Example: my /mī/

Read the one-syllable words below. Write the sound the vowel makes on the line.

10. shy _____
11. me _____
12. by _____
13. go _____
14. fly _____
15. cry _____

Now use three of the words above in sentences of your own.

16. _____
17. _____
18. _____

Name _____

More Open Syllables

Fill in each line with the word from the box that best completes the sentence.

| my | me | cry | flu | I | she | go | try | fly |

1. Ron is sick with the _____.

2. _____ likes to wear her black dress.

3. Lian and _____ will _____ in a plane.

4. Juan will _____ to pass the test.

5. Dad likes to read to Jack and _____.

6. The small children will _____ if they are scared.

7. There is mud on _____ blue shoes.

8. Do not _____ near the train tracks.

Write the long vowel sound on the line next to each word below.

9. he /___/   sly /___/   hi /___/   pro /___/   flu /___/

10. me /___/   no /___/   ply /___/   so /___/   by /___/

Long Vowels/Open Syllables

When "Y" Sounds Like Long "E"

When the vowel **y** is at the end of a word with more than one syllable, the **y** often has a long **e** sound.

On the lines, write the word that names the picture. The first letter of each word has been given to help you.

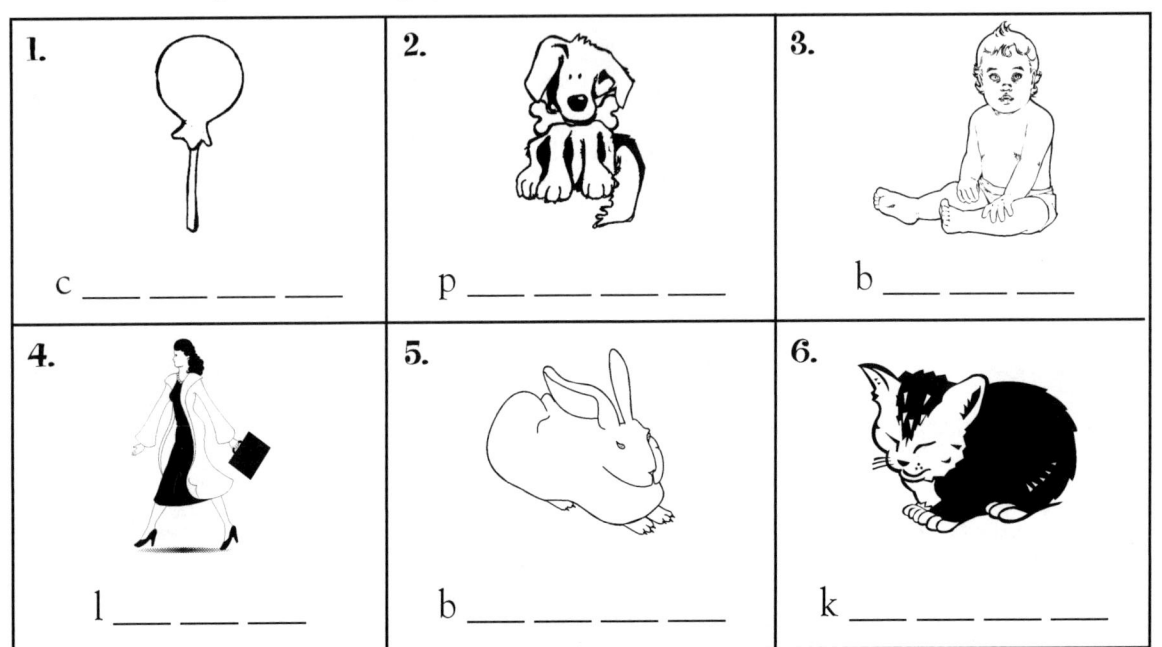

1. c __ __ __	2. p __ __ __ __	3. b __ __ __
4. l __ __ __	5. b __ __ __ __	6. k __ __ __ __

Combine the following syllables to make words ending in **y**.

7. ti + dy = _____

8. ru + by = _____

9. san + dy = _____

10. plen + ty = _____

Separate the words into syllables. Mark the long vowels.

Example: baby /bā bē/

11. silly = _____

12. hobby = _____

13. funny = _____

14. holly = _____

15. happy = _____

16. penny = _____

Long Vowels/Open Syllables

Name _____

Ends with "Y"

Fill in each line with the word from the box that best completes the sentence. **Remember:** When the letter **y** comes at the end of a word with two or more syllables, it usually sounds like long **e**.

funny	ruby	Molly	buddy	lady
fifty	lazy	sandy	messy	sunny

1. Roz has a new _____ ring.

2. Ted and _____ went to a great movie!

3. The _____ will wear a red dress.

4. It is warm and _____ today.

5. Sam is my best _____.

6. Brad will clean his _____ room.

7. Cliff is too _____ to do the work that is needed.

8. At the party, Pat laughed at a _____ clown.

9. The beach is rocky and _____.

10. On Jim's next birthday, he will be _____.

Long Vowels/Open Syllables

Names Ending in "Y"

The following names have a **y** ending that sounds like long **e**. **Remember:** When the letter **y** comes at the end of a word with two or more syllables, it usually sounds like a long **e**.

Example: Benny   /Ben nē/

Divide the following names into syllables. Write a long **e** for the **y**.

1. Billy   = _____
2. Sammy = _____
3. Mandy   = _____
4. Tommy = _____
5. Missy   = _____
6. Cody   = _____
7. Toby   = _____
8. Molly   = _____
9. Tony   = _____
10. Mindy = _____

Combine the following syllables to make names.

11. Bet sē = _____
12. Kris sē = _____
13. Hol lē = _____
14. Rob bē = _____
15. Sal lē = _____
16. Bob bē = _____
17. Jen nē = _____
18. Pat tē = _____
19. Peg gē = _____
20. Ju dē   = _____

Name _____

The Silent "E"

The **silent e** follows a pattern of **consonant-vowel-consonant-e (CVCe)** or **vowel-consonant-e (VCe)**. Even though many words with **silent e** begin with a consonant, it is easier just to remember **VCe** as a clue when reading and spelling words with the **silent e.** Note the pattern in the following keywords.

    Examples: a as in *cāke*; e as in *Pēte*; i as in *bīke*;
    o as in *hōme*; u as in *mūle* and *tūbe*

In these words, the letter **e** makes the vowel before the consonant-e long. With this kind of pattern, the **e** at the end of the syllable is silent.

Change the **CVC**-syllable words with short vowel sounds to **VCe**-syllable words with long vowel sounds. Mark the short vowels in the words below, and then mark the long vowels in the words you write on the lines. Remember to cross out the **silent e.** The first one has been done for you.

1. căp + e = ____cāpe____
2. cub + e = _____
3. tub + e = _____
4. dim + e = _____
5. hid + e = _____
6. bit + e = _____
7. can + e = _____
8. cop + e = _____
9. hop + e = _____
10. rid + e = _____
11. cut + e = _____
12. hat + e = _____
13. scrap + e = _____
14. strip + e = _____
15. slid + e = _____
16. plan + e = _____
17. slop + e = _____
18. spin + e = _____

Silent *e*

Daily Skill-Builders Spelling & Phonics 4–5
walch.com © 2004 Walch Publishing

Shh! Silent "E"

On the lines, write the **silent-e** word that names the picture. The first letter of each word has been given to help you.

1. p _ _ _ _ _	2. b _ _ _	3. n _ _ _
4. m _ _ _	5. s _ _ _ _	6. h _ _ _ _
7. c _ _ _ _	8. b _ _ _	9. f _ _ _ _
10. c _ _ _	11. p _ _ _ _ _	12. f _ _ _

Name _____

A Word or Not a Word?

Cross out the **silent e** at the end of each word below. If the letters still make a word without the **silent e,** write the new word on the line. If not, leave it blank. The first one has been done for you.

A	1. ap~~e~~ _____ 2. plane _____ 3. maze _____ 4. safe _____	hat~~e~~ __hat__ scrape _____ cane _____ brave _____
I	5. dive _____ 6. spine _____ 7. life _____ 8. bite _____	slide _____ bike _____ mile _____ dime _____
O	9. hope _____ 10. home _____ 11. vote _____ 12. cope _____	bone _____ phone _____ globe _____ broke _____
U	13. tune _____ 14. cute _____ 15. mule _____ 16. tube _____	cube _____ rule _____ prune _____ flute _____

Silent e

Name _____

Breaking Even More Rules

Usually, when words and syllables follow a **VCe** pattern, the first vowel sound is long and the **e** is silent, such as in the word *cake*. Some words in this pattern do not carry a long vowel sound in the first vowel, as in *give* and *love*.

Rulebreaker: ive and **ove** do not always have a long vowel sound.

The letters **ive** can have a long or a short vowel **i** sound. The letter **e** is still silent.

Read these words with the letters **ive**. Write the short or long sound of **i** on each line.

Examples: give = ĭ   drive = ī

1. olive = _____
2. dive = _____
3. five = _____
4. active = _____
5. jive = _____
6. live = _____

  * The word **live** can be read two ways.

The letters **ove** can have a long ō or short ŭ sound. The letter **e** is silent.

Read the following **ove** words. Write the sound of **o** after each word.

Examples: love = ŭ   cove = ō

7. above = _____
8. stove = _____
9. love = _____
10. grove = _____

Silent *e*

Name _____

When "S" Sounds Like "Z"

The letter **s** can sound like a **z** when it comes at the end of a word, especially when it is in a **silent-e** word (**VCe**).

   Example: wise /wīz/

Read the following words, and say the **z** sound in place of the **s** sound before the **silent e**. Write what the word sounds like on the line using the letter **z**. Be sure to mark the vowels.

1. nose   /___/
2. hose   /___/
3. wise   /___/
4. rise   /___/
5. rose   /___/
6. these /___/
7. those /___/
8. pose   /___/
9. fuse   /___/
10. use   /___/

Fill in each line with the word from the box that best completes the sentence.

| wise | rise | use | nose | hose | rose | pose |

11. Ellie fell on the pavement and scraped her _____.

12. Ross gave Maria a long-stem _____.

13. Can you _____ for a picture?

14. The bread will _____ in the oven.

15. It is _____ to complete all your homework.

16. The firefighter will _____ a _____ on the fire.

Silent *e*

Searching for Silent "E"

In the word search, circle only the words from the box that have a **silent e**. Words can be found vertically, horizontally, diagonally, or backwards.

cat	cute	bite	bat	bone	flute
bike	pan	pin	fame	hat	fast
cake	here	care	pine	clone	plane

```
S W E R R C I H M P L E D A
F C C E D F S E E W R E X H
H A D P X M N T W D T J C P
L K F X X O U B S I N S R N
P E P E B L X U B O K E G G
N S L N F N W G X R N R B C
C H A I H L B A C I X A N U
A W N P P Q X G E E C C F P
I R E U A C O L J U L R A I
L Y T A E W R S T W L W M S
M M W R A V Y E T P M B E D
B K E B I F C S E N O L C Q
O H K C J E K I B H Q R Y P
O W G T C X O N U E Q A P M
```

Name _____

More Than One

Many words have two **closed syllables**. (**Remember:** In these words, the vowel sounds are short because they are closed in by one or more consonants.) The words below have syllables that follow a **CVC** or **VC** pattern.

Read the words below and divide them into syllables.

Examples: uphill = up + hill   sunset = sun + set

1. contest = _____ _____
2. combat = _____ _____
3. himself = _____ _____
4. finish = _____ _____
5. public = _____ _____
6. suffix = _____ _____
7. dentist = _____ _____
8. tablet = _____ _____
9. napkin = _____ _____
10. pumpkin = _____ _____
11. trumpet = _____ _____
12. snapshot = _____ _____
13. witness = _____ _____
14. express = _____ _____
15. chipmunk = _____ _____

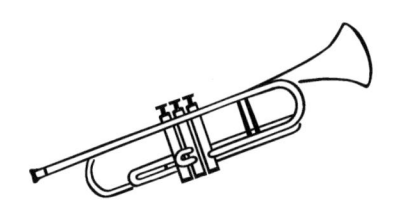

Words with Two Closed Syllables

Name

Adding Closed Syllables

Add the following syllables to make words. Then read the words. Mark all the vowels. The first one has been done for you.

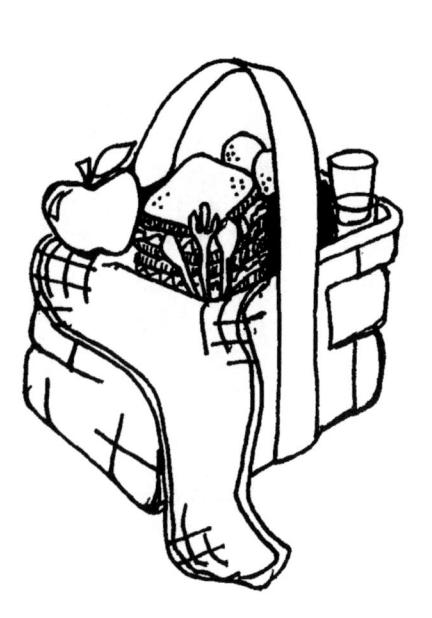

1. pic + nic = _____pĭcnĭc_____

2. tal + ent = _____

3. sum + mit = _____

4. ton + sil = _____

5. prob + lem = _____

6. cob + web = _____

7. un + pack = _____

8. can + not = _____

9. plas + tic = _____

10. fos + sil = _____

11. pump + kin = _____

12. con + test = _____

Daily Skill-Builders Spelling & Phonics 4–5
walch.com © 2004 Walch Publishing

Words with Two Closed Syllables

Name

Two-Syllable Words

On the lines, write the word that names the picture. The first letter of each word has been given to help you.

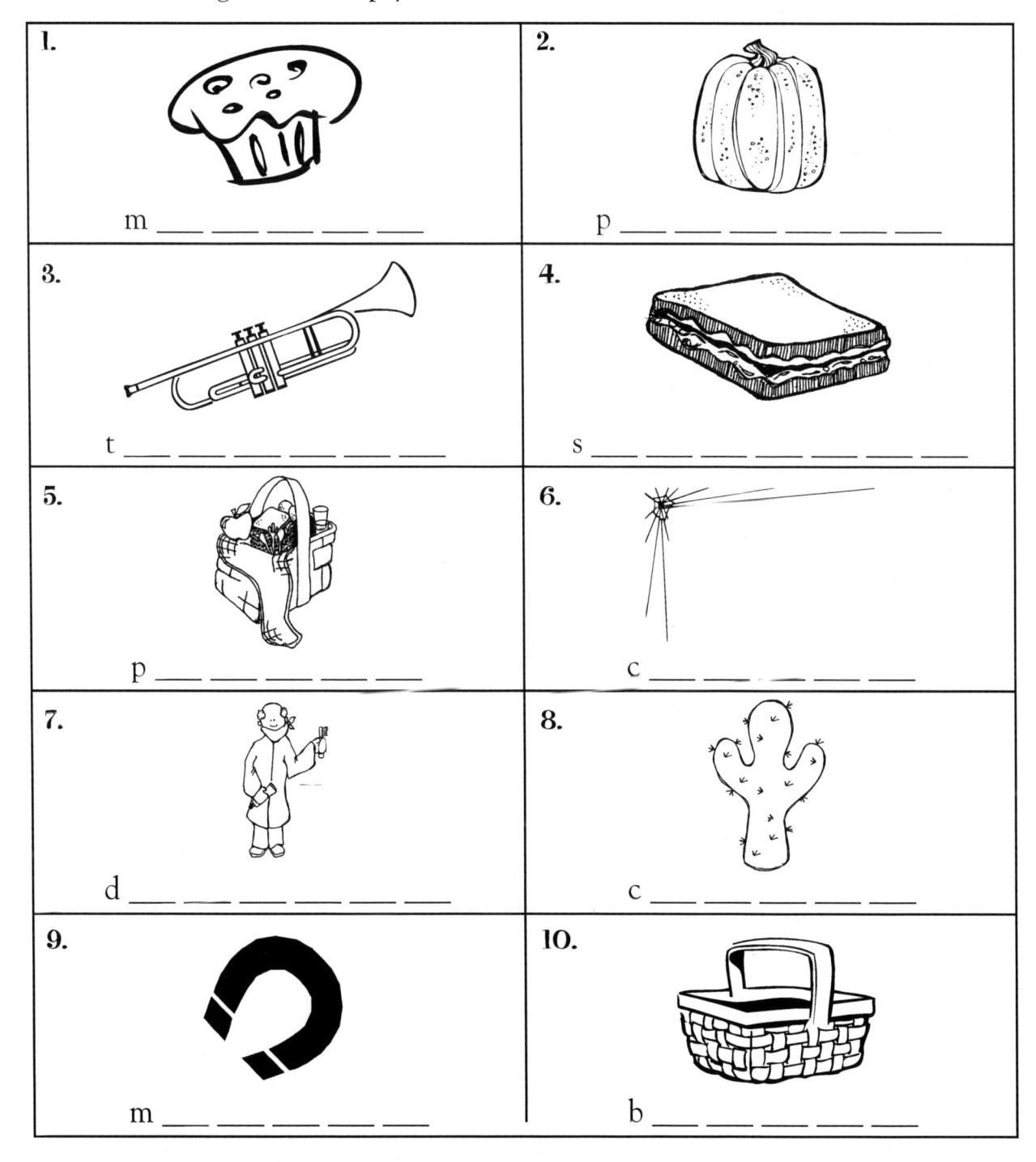

1. m _ _ _ _ _ _

2. p _ _ _ _ _ _ _

3. t _ _ _ _ _ _ _

4. s _ _ _ _ _ _ _ _

5. p _ _ _ _ _ _

6. c _ _ _ _ _ _

7. d _ _ _ _ _ _

8. c _ _ _ _ _ _

9. m _ _ _ _ _ _

10. b _ _ _ _ _ _

Words with Two Closed Syllables

Daily Skill-Builders Spelling & Phonics 4–5
walch.com © 2004 Walch Publishing

Name _____

Complete the Sentences

The words in the box have two syllables that follow a **CVC** or **VC** pattern. Fill in each line with the word from the box that best completes the sentence.

pumpkin	pollen	sandwich	unpack	contest
problem	unlock	cotton	picnic	hopscotch

1. Elizabeth can do every math _____.

2. Please _____ your suitcase.

3. _____ the back door so I can get in.

4. Missy will carve the _____ for the Halloween party.

5. The _____ makes me sneeze every summer.

6. I can't wait to attend the family _____.

7. Did you play _____ on the pavement?

8. My soft shirt is made of _____.

9. Sammy won the swimming _____.

10. My favorite kind of _____ is peanut butter and jelly.

Name _____

Making It Real

Connect the closed syllables to make words by drawing lines in each box.

1.
den	nic
pic	tist
ob	pet
trum	ject

2.
pump	not
can	kin
hap	sip
gos	pen

3. Write the words from above on the lines below.

_____ _____ _____ _____

_____ _____ _____ _____

Use five words from above in sentences of your own.

4. _____

5. _____

6. _____

7. _____

8. _____

Words with Two Closed Syllables

Name _____

Three-Syllable Words

Here are some three-syllable words with the **CVC** or **VC** pattern in each syllable.

Examples: pun + ish + ment = pŭnĭshmĕnt
ath + let + ic = ăthlĕtĭc

Combine the following syllables to make words. Then mark the vowels.

1. fan + tas + tic = _____

2. in + hab + it = _____

3. bas + ket + ball = _____

4. pen + man + ship = _____

5. mag + net + ic = _____

6. Wis + con + sin = _____

7. crafts + man + ship = _____

8. Thanks + giv + ing = _____

9. con + sis + tent = _____

10. dis + in + fect = _____

68 Daily Skill-Builders Spelling & Phonics 4–5
walch.com © 2004 Walch Publishing

Words with Three Closed Syllables

Name _____

Syllable Division

Many words have combined syllables such as **VC, CVC,** and **VCe** (**silent-e**) patterns.

Examples: homesick = home + sick   inflate = in + flate

Divide the following words into syllables.

1. inhale = _____ + _____
2. exhale = _____ + _____
3. invite = _____ + _____
4. tadpole = _____ + _____
5. trombone = _____ + _____
6. cupcake = _____ + _____
7. turnpike = _____ + _____
8. bedtime = _____ + _____
9. dislike = _____ + _____
10. costume = _____ + _____
11. inside = _____ + _____
12. baseball = _____ + _____
13. springtime = _____ + _____
14. milkshake = _____ + _____
15. pancake = _____ + _____
16. mistake = _____ + _____
17. explode = _____ + _____
18. basement = _____ + _____

Closed Syllables and Silent *e*

Finish Your Sentence

Fill in each line with the word from the box that best completes the sentence.

baseball	turnpike	trombone	homesick
escape	tadpole	combine	fireman
costume	pancake	airplane	improve

1. Today I'm going to try to catch a(n) _____ in the pond.

2. My sister plays the _____ in her school band.

3. My mom has to take the _____ to get to work every day.

4. Lock your hamster in its cage so it doesn't _____.

5. We are taking a(n) _____ when we go on vacation this year.

6. Will you make me a(n) _____ for breakfast?

7. When you _____ oil and water, it separates.

8. A(n) _____ came to our school to teach us about fire safety.

9. My brother gets _____ when he goes away to soccer camp.

10. In gym class today, we played _____.

11. I haven't decided what to wear for a Halloween _____.

12. Every day I practice so that I will _____.

Closed Syllables and Silent *e*

Name _____

Syllable Combinations

Combine the syllables to make words. Mark the vowels. Then draw a line to connect the word to the picture that matches it.

1. rep + tile
   _____

2. cup + cake
   _____

3. fire + man
   _____

4. trom + bone
   _____

5. pan + cake
   _____

6. base + ball
   _____

7. cos + tume
   _____

8. milk + shake
   _____

Closed Syllables and Silent *e*

Daily Skill-Builders Spelling & Phonics 4–5
walch.com © 2004 Walch Publishing

Name _____

Connect the Syllables

Connect the syllables in each box below by drawing lines to make words.

1.
mis	hale
care	cake
ex	take
pan	less

2.
spring	safe
un	time
dis	sick
home	like

3. Write the words from above on the lines below.

_____   _____
_____   _____
_____   _____
_____   _____

Use five words from above in sentences of your own.

4. _____

5. _____

6. _____

7. _____

8. _____

72 Daily Skill-Builders Spelling & Phonics 4–5
walch.com © 2004 Walch Publishing

Closed Syllables and Silent *e*

Name _____

More Three-Syllable Words

Here are some three-syllable words with combined **CVC**, **VC**, and **VCe (silent-e)** syllables.

Examples: văl + ĕn + tīnẹ = valentine   cŏn + trĭb + ūtẹ = contribute

Read and combine the following syllables to make words. Mark the vowels long or short. Remember to cross out each **silent e**.

1. rec + og + nize = _____

2. dem + on + strate = _____

3. in + com + plete = _____

4. dis + trib + ute = _____

5. con + tem + plate = _____

Fill in each line with the word from the box that best completes the sentence.

6. The teacher will _____ _____ how to solve the math problem.

7. Please _____ the papers to all the students.

8. Do not leave your homework _____.

9. The students did not _____ the new teacher.

10. We will _____ the meaning of the story.

Closed Syllables and Silent *e*

Daily Skill-Builders Spelling & Phonics 4–5
walch.com © 2004 Walch Publishing

Name _____

Open and Closed

The following words have a combination of open and closed syllables. **Remember:** Open syllables end in vowels (**CV** pattern) and have long vowel sounds. Closed syllables end in consonants (**CVC** or **VC** pattern) and usually have short vowel sounds.

Examples: tulip = tū + lĭp   banjo = băn + jō

Sometimes an open syllable has only one vowel in it.

Examples: open = ō + pĕn   evil = ē + vĭl

Read and combine the following syllables to make words. Mark the vowels long or short.

1. se + cret = _____
2. be + gan = _____
3. pre + tend = _____
4. fro + zen = _____
5. my + self = _____
6. re + lax = _____
7. ho + tel = _____
8. mo + tel = _____
9. stu + dent = _____
10. hu + mid = _____
11. spo + ken = _____
12. ro + dent = _____

74 *Daily Skill-Builders* Spelling & Phonics 4–5
walch.com © 2004 Walch Publishing

Open and Closed Syllables

Name _____

Banjo Music

Do you know the types of syllables in the words in the title of this page? There is a combination of open and closed syllables. Open syllables end in vowels and have long vowel sounds. Closed syllables end in consonants and usually have short vowel sounds.

Divide the syllables in the following words, and mark the vowels long or short.

1. banjo = _____ + _____   2. music = _____ + _____

Fill in each line with the word from the box that best completes the sentence.

| banjo | music | student | hotel |
| begin | relax | frozen | mason |

3. The _____ sang a solo in _____ class.

4. The play will _____ when the curtain goes up.

5. I'll go ice skating when the lake is _____.

6. The _____ used bricks to make a path.

7. I like to _____ by the pool.

8. Carson plays the _____ in his band.

9. We will stay at a _____ on our vacation.

Open and Closed Syllables

Daily Skill-Builders Spelling & Phonics 4–5
walch.com © 2004 Walch Publishing

75

Name _____

Open or Closed?

In the word search, circle only the words from the box with one open syllable and one closed syllable. Words can be found vertically, horizontally, diagonally, and backwards.

began	cupcake	behind	finish	even	pretend
napkin	myself	solo	open	motel	hero
frozen	relax	human	rewind	necklace	tulip

```
W I B T E D S P R A W L V T
Y F M I S W Z P A N D A J L
M R B Y C S Y P E Q Q S Y I
G O E T S Y B V O P E N O M
I Z G U N E E H N R P A G H
B E A L D A L R E W I N D S
A N N I H N M F Q H Q A D Q
S I W P D L I U E F N N K P
T R A I E N B H H U E N R R
P R R T Y D V I E T U E O D
W A O W G I M I E B L T M S
M M H D M U I R U A V I C A
O H B Q H L P I X Q H D V U
I G D W B Q P J O C A M D R
```

Name _____

More Open Syllables

Some words have more than one open syllable. Open syllables end in vowels and have long vowel sounds.

Example: hero = hē + rō

Many words with more than one open syllable end in the letter **y** and often have the long **e** sound.

Example: holy = hō + ly /lē/

Combine the following open syllables to make words. Be sure to mark the vowels. Write in the **y** sound. The first one has been done for you.

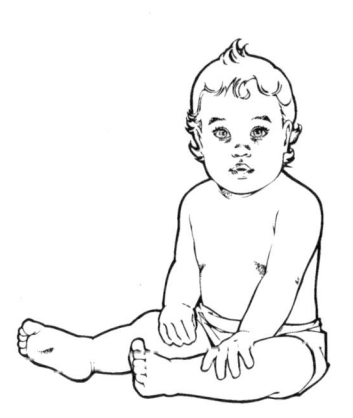

1. la + dy = _lādy /dē/_

2. si + lo = _____

3. ze + ro = _____

4. e + mu = _____

5. ba + by = _____

6. ha + lo = _____

7. bo + ny = _____

8. cra + zy = _____

9. so + lo = _____

10. ru + by = _____

Words with Two Open Syllables

Name _____

Open-Syllable Words

All of the words below have two open syllables that end with long vowel sounds. **Remember:** The **y** at the end of a word with multiple syllables often sounds like the long **e.**

Divide the following words by their open syllables.

1. holy = _____ + _____
2. hero = _____ + _____
3. veto = _____ + _____
4. tiny = _____ + _____
5. navy = _____ + _____
6. zero = _____ + _____
7. halo = _____ + _____
8. baby = _____ + _____
9. tidy = _____ + _____
10. emu = _____ + _____
11. tutu = _____ + _____
12. pony = _____ + _____
13. hazy = _____ + _____
14. solo = _____ + _____

Now use four of the words above in sentences of your own.

15. _____
16. _____
17. _____
18. _____

Name _____

Open and Silent "E"

Many words have a combination of open syllables (**CV** pattern) and **silent-e** syllables (**VCe** pattern). Look at the syllable types in these two-syllable words.

Examples: locate = lō + cāte̸   beside = bē + sīde̸

Read and combine the following syllables to make words. Mark the vowels long or short. Remember to cross out the **silent e**.

1. de + cide = _____
2. pro + mote = _____
3. o + zone = _____
4. ro + tate = _____
5. lo + cate = _____
6. be + side = _____
7. po + lite = _____
8. be + have = _____
9. mi + grate = _____
10. re + mote = _____

Fill in each line with the word from above that best completes the sentence.

11. I want to change the channel, but I can't find the _____.

12. That little girl is so _____. She's always saying "please" and "thank you."

13. Most of the birds around here _____ south for the winter.

14. I can't _____ whether I want to rent a movie or go to a movie tonight.

15. Please _____ for the babysitter while I am gone.

Open Syllables and Silent e

It Ends with "LE"

Another syllable type has a consonant and the letters **le**. The **le** has the /l/ sound and a **silent e**.

Examples: ap + ple = apple   ma + ple = maple

In the word *apple*, the first syllable has a short vowel sound because it ends with a consonant. In the word *maple*, the first syllable has a long vowel sound because it ends with a vowel. Both words have a consonant and **le** in the last syllable.

Combine the following syllables to make words. Write the word on the first line. On the second line, write whether the first syllable in the word is long or short. The first one has been done for you.

1. ta + ble = _____table_____   _____long_____
2. can + dle = _____   _____
3. lit + tle = _____   _____
4. ti + tle = _____   _____
5. puz + zle = _____   _____
6. ca + ble = _____   _____
7. bot + tle = _____   _____
8. mid + dle = _____   _____
9. no + ble = _____   _____
10. sam + ple = _____   _____

Separating "LE"

Read the following words that contain the consonant + **le** pattern. Divide the words into syllables. The first one has been done for you.

1. waffle   waf   fle
2. pickle _____ _____
3. maple _____ _____
4. uncle _____ _____
5. simple _____ _____
6. puzzle _____ _____
7. cable _____ _____
8. muscle _____ _____
9. chuckle _____ _____
10. fiddle _____ _____

Read the following sentences. Circle the **le** words. Then write the words on the lines, dividing them into syllables.

11. That baby has a cute little dimple in one cheek.

    _____ _____

12. The title of this book is "Drizzle in the Jungle."

    _____ _____ _____

13. Please buckle your seatbelts and settle down for the ride.

    _____ _____

14. Will you light the candle on that table?

    _____ _____

15. Are you able to whistle?

    _____ _____

le Syllable

Name _____

"S" or "Z" Sound?

Often a new word can be formed by adding **-s** to a base word. The word *shop* is a base word. If the letter **-s** is added to it, then the word becomes plural.

Example: shop + s = shop**s**

Combine the base words below with the ending **-s** to make new words. Sometimes the letter **-s** at the end of a word has a *z* sound, such as in the word *bags*. After writing each new word, write the sound of **-s,** either /s/ or /z/.

1. flame + s = _____ /___/
2. bat + s = _____ /___/
3. sing + s = _____ /___/
4. hop + s = _____ /___/
5. ship + s = _____ /___/
6. cane + s = _____ /___/
7. flute + s = _____ /___/
8. dad + s = _____ /___/
9. hug + s = _____ /___/
10. hill + s = _____ /___/
11. bike + s = _____ /___/
12. snake + s = _____ /___/
13. help + s = _____ /___/
14. bath + s = _____ /___/
15. handcuff + s = _____ /___/
16. reptile + s = _____ /___/
17. vampire + s = _____ /___/
18. handshake + s = _____ /___/
19. flagpole + s = _____ /___/
20. cupcake + s = _____ /___/

Name _____

Making It Plural

Adding an **-s** to a noun (person, place, or thing) is one way to make a word plural.

   Example: stripe + s = stripes

On the line, write the word that names the picture. Add an **-s** to make it plural.

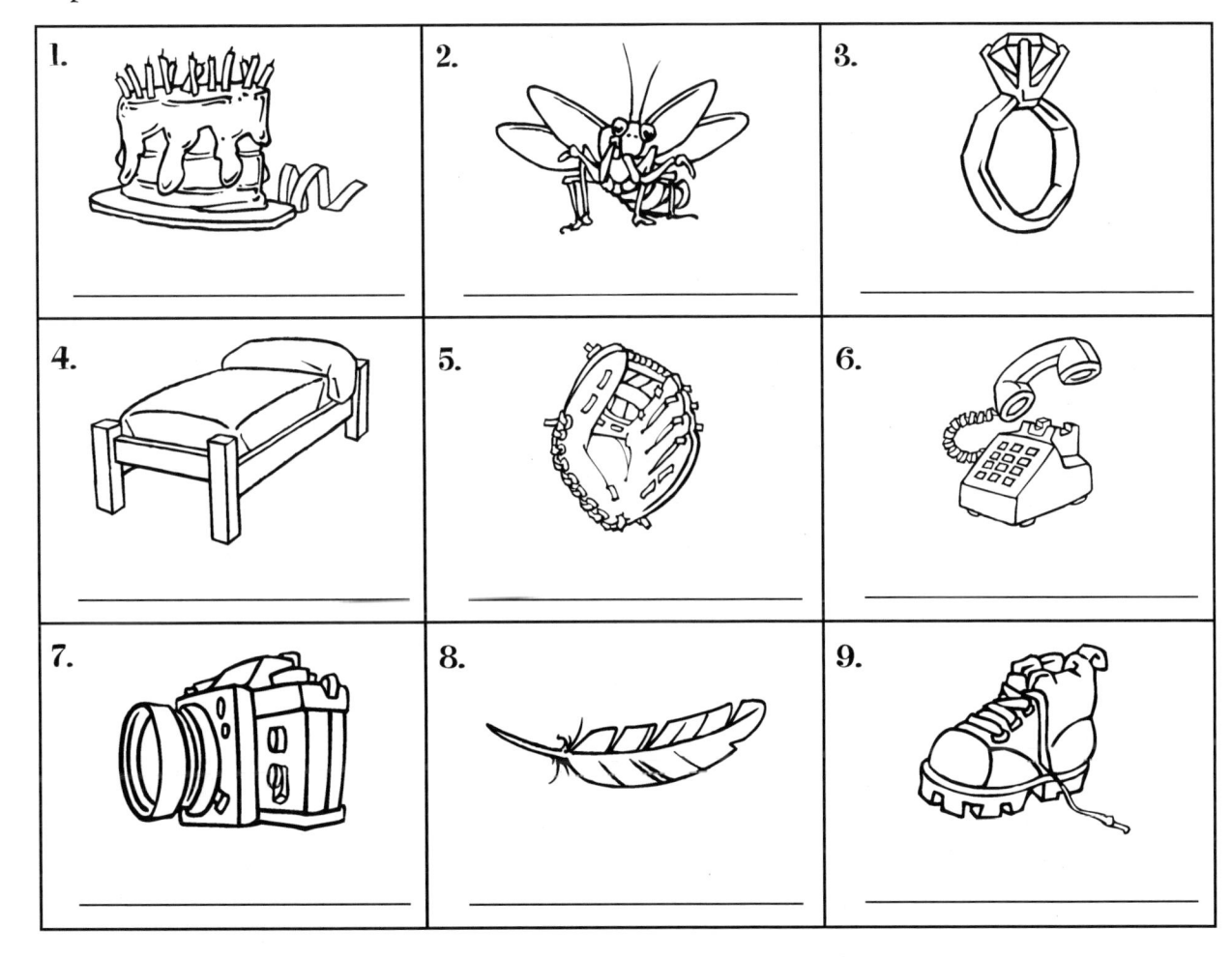

1. _____	2. _____	3. _____
4. _____	5. _____	6. _____
7. _____	8. _____	9. _____

Use two of the words above in sentences of your own.

10. _____

11. _____

Plurals with **-s**

Name _____

When to Add "ES"

The ending -es sounds like /iz/. You can add -es to base words ending in the letters **s, x, z, sh, ch, tch.**

Examples: dress + es = dresses   box + es = boxes
buzz + es = buzzes   dish + es = dishes
rich + es = riches   batch + es = batches

Add the ending -es to the following base words. Then read the new words.
Remember: The sound of -es is /iz/.

1. tax___   lunch___   match___   brush___   mess___

2. ax___   bench___   witch___   splash___   miss___

3. box___   munch___   crutch___   wish___   fuss___

4. fix___   inch___   stitch___   flash___   boss___

Use four plural words from above in sentences of your own.

5. _____

6. _____

7. _____

8. _____

Name _____

Adding "S" or "ES"

On the line, write the word that names the picture. Add an **-s** or an **-es** to make the word plural.

1. _____	2. _____	3. _____
4. _____	5. _____	6. _____
7. _____	8. _____	9. _____
10. _____	11. _____	12. _____

Plurals with *-s* and *-es*

Daily Skill-Builders Spelling & Phonics 4–5
walch.com © 2004 Walch Publishing

Name _____

"S" or "ES"?

Add **-s** or **-es** to the following words. Then rewrite the words.

1. dish + ___ = _____

2. mug + ___ = _____

3. rich + ___ = _____

4. bus + ___ = _____

5. song + ___ = _____

6. fall + ___ = _____

7. pinch + ___ = _____

8. guess + ___ = _____

9. bike + ___ = _____

10. play + ___ = _____

11. box + ___ = _____

12. rash + ___ = _____

Daily Skill-Builders Spelling & Phonics 4–5
walch.com © 2004 Walch Publishing

Plurals with -s and -es

Name _____

"Y" to "I"

When forming the plural of a word that ends in **y**, change the **y** to **i** and add **-es**. If a vowel comes before the **y**, just add **-s**.

    Example: toy + s = toy**s**

If there is one or more consonants before the **y**, change the **y** to **i** and add **-es**.

    Example: puppy + es = pupp**ies**
               The **y** is gone, and now there is an **i** in its place.

Write the plural form of each word below in the correct column.

city	key	party	country	agency
donkey	holiday	play	chimney	spy
enemy	company	duty	Monday	boy

1.   y to i + -es   2.   add -es

_____   _____
_____   _____
_____   _____
_____   _____
_____   _____
_____   _____
_____   _____

Plurals: Changing *y* to *i*

Name _____

It Ends in "O"

Words that end in **o** form their plurals by adding **-s** or **-es**. Add **-s** to words that have vowels before the **o**.

Example: radio + **s** = radio**s**

Words that have a consonant before the **o** may end in **-s** or **-es**. Check a dictionary if you are unsure.

Examples: photo + **s** = photo**s**   potato + **es** = potato**es**

Complete each sentence below by writing the plural form of the word under the line.

1. _____ are my favorite type of animal.
   kangaroo

2. Please don't put any _____ on my sandwich.
   tomato

3. I have never seen so many _____ in one room before.
   piano

4. _____ live in _____, which are
   Eskimo   igloo
   made of ice.

5. My mom and my grandfather are my _____.
   hero

6. There were so many _____ at the store that I
   radio
   couldn't decide which one I wanted.

7. My dad went to a lot of _____ when he was in Texas
   rodeo
   on vacation.

8. My uncle repairs old _____ in his spare time.
   stereo

Name _____

From "F" to "V"

To form the plural of words that end in **f** or **fe**, change the **f** or **fe** to **v** and add **-es.**

Examples: calf + es = cal**ves**   knife + es = kni**ves**
The **f** is gone, and now there is a **v** in its place.

Read the words below. Write the plural form of the word on the line.

1. elf _____
2. loaf _____
3. wife _____
4. half _____
5. leaf _____
6. life _____
7. shelf _____
8. scarf _____

Fill in each line with the word from above that best completes the sentence. Be sure to use the correct form (singular or plural) so that the sentence makes sense.

9. We buy two _____ of bread each week at the bakery.

10. I usually wear a _____ in the winter to keep my neck warm.

11. Every autumn we rake the _____ into piles and jump in them.

12. The only books we can take home are the ones on that _____.

13. People say that cats have nine _____.

14. Please break that candy bar into two _____ and share it with your sister.

Plurals: Changing *f* to *v*

Name _____

So Irregular

The plural forms of some words are made by changing the spellings of their singular forms.

Example: man (singular) ⟶ men (plural)

The plural forms of some words can be the same as their singular forms.

Example: deer (singular and plural)

Write the plural form of each word on the line. Check a dictionary if needed.

1. child _____
2. moose _____
3. woman _____
4. tooth _____
5. fish _____
6. mouse _____
7. sheep _____
8. foot _____
9. goose _____
10. reindeer _____

Fill in each line with the word from above that best completes the sentence. Be sure to use the correct form (singular or plural) so that the sentence makes sense.

11. I have lost almost all of my baby _____, and my adult ones have grown in their place.

12. One of my _____ is bigger than the other, so I have a hard time fitting into shoes.

13. There are six other _____ in my dance class.

14. Most of the _____ in my tank hide behind the plants so you can't usually see them.

15. I didn't know that the wool in my sweater came from _____.

Name _____

Reviewing Plurals

Write the plural form of each word on the line.

1. radio _____ 2. party _____

3. scarf _____ 4. moose _____

5. holiday _____ 6. knife _____

7. mouse _____ 8. hero _____

9. baby _____ 10. tooth _____

11. igloo _____ 12. half _____

13. stereo _____ 14. donkey _____

15. calf _____ 16. foot _____

17. woman _____ 18. kangaroo _____

19. enemy _____ 20. life _____

Plurals: Review

Daily Skill-Builders Spelling & Phonics 4–5
walch.com © 2004 Walch Publishing

91

Name _____

"ING" Action

The ending -ing can be added to many base words to form new words.

   Example: walk + **ing** = walk**ing**

Circle the base words in the following **-ing** words.

1. fishing   boxing   resting   singing   sleeping
2. jumping   adding   yelling   golfing   thinking
3. banking   bringing   packing   selling   missing

Fill in each line with the word from above that best completes the sentence.

4. When my dad and I go _____, we always wear our life jackets on the boat.

5. Stop _____ at me! The neighbors can probably hear you.

6. My mom always tells us to stop _____ on our beds.

7. Be quiet when you go into the house because the baby is _____.

8. My homework is _____! I can't find it anywhere.

9. We have to finish _____ because we are leaving for our vacation tomorrow.

10. I can tell when my grandmother is in a good mood because she is always _____.

Name _____

Adding "ING" to Silent "E"

When adding the ending **-ing** to **silent-e** words (**VCe** pattern), drop the **e** before adding **ing.**

   Example: love + ing = lov**ing**

Add **ing** to the **silent-e** words below. Make sure to drop the **e** when writing the word on the line.

1. bake + ing = _____
2. make + ing = _____
3. bike + ing = _____
4. hope + ing = _____
5. give + ing = _____
6. dive + ing = _____

Look at the following **-ing** words. Write the base word on the line.

7. joking _____
8. saving _____
9. shining _____
10. rising _____
11. moving _____
12. shaking _____

Fill in each line with the word from above that best completes the sentence.

13. I am _____ my money for a new mountain bike.

14. We are _____ into our new house next week.

15. I am _____ to finish this book before going to see the movie.

16. I love _____ off the dock at the lake in the summer.

17. The sun is _____ and there's not a cloud in the sky.

18. We usually go _____ on the trails behind our house.

Name _____

Finishing Sentences

Fill in each line with the **-ing** word from the box that best completes the sentence.

golfing	jumping	making	resting	baking
folding	dressing	locking	hiking	living

1. My dad pulled his clubs out of the garage, so I knew he was going _____.

2. The mother was _____ her baby after she changed his diaper.

3. The children were _____ on the trampoline.

4. Mom was _____ in her chair after a long day of work.

5. The guard was _____ the bank doors at 5:00 P.M.

6. The towels needed _____ after they were washed and dried.

7. Pete likes to go _____ on the mountain trails.

8. I love _____ chocolate chip cookies with my mom.

9. I will eat my breakfast after _____ my bed.

Name _____

Adding "ING" to CVC Words

When adding the ending **-ing** to base words that follow a consonant-vowel-consonant (**CVC**) pattern, double the last consonant of the word. This works when there is only one consonant at the end of the word.

Example: swim + **ing** = swimm**ing**

Add **-ing** to the following words. Be sure to double the last consonant if necessary. Write the **-ing** word on the line.

1. nap _____
2. run _____
3. shop _____
4. hop _____

Look at the following **-ing** words. Write the base word on the line. Be careful to remember the rules for adding **-ing.**

5. hoping _____
6. banking _____
7. sledding _____
8. loving _____
9. shipping _____
10. walking _____
11. biking _____
12. chatting _____

Look at the following **-ing** words. Some are spelled correctly, and some are not. If the word is spelled correctly, write **C** for **correct** on the line. If it is misspelled, write **M** for **misspelled.** Then write the correct spelling on the line.

13. quiting _____
14. bakeing _____
15. hugging _____
16. tapping _____
17. writting _____
18. jumpping _____

Ending *-ing*

Daily Skill-Builders Spelling & Phonics 4–5
walch.com © 2004 Walch Publishing

Name _____

Put It in the Past

The ending **-ed** is added to words to show past tense. It has three sounds.

> When **-ed** is added to some words, it makes the /ed/ sound.
>
> **Example:** lift + **ed** = lift**ed**
>
> When **-ed** is added to some words, it makes the /d/ sound.
>
> **Example:** belong + **ed** = belong**ed**
>
> When **-ed** is added to some words, it makes the /t/ sound.
>
> **Example:** thank + **ed** = thank**ed**

In the box below, circle the words that make the /ed/ sound. Underline the words that make the /t/ sound. Draw a box around the words that make the /d/ sound. Then, choose a word from the box that best completes each sentence.

yelled	brushed	called	stamped	wished
folded	rested	hunted	twisted	crossed
melted	dunked	pretended	distracted	disrupted

1. I _____ to be a fairy godmother and granted my sister's wish.

2. My mother _____ the butter in the pan to make the cookies.

3. My brother _____ for a toy truck for his birthday.

4. I started talking in class without raising my hand, and my teacher said that I _____ class.

5. Jenny _____ the laundry in the basket.

Name _____

What Do You Hear?

The ending **-ed** has three sounds: /ed/, /d/, and /t/.

Read the sentences below. After each **-ed** word, write the sound **-ed** makes.

1. We yelled /__/ to my brother from the car and honked /__/ the horn.

2. My mother pressed /__/ and folded /__/ the laundry.

3. The man at the gate stamped /__/ our hands so we could get back into the park.

4. I called /__/ Jamie and asked /__/ her what we were assigned for homework.

5. Last summer, my friends and I camped /__/ in my backyard.

6. I spelled /__/ a lot of words wrong in my story.

7. I woke my grandmother up when I laughed /__/, but I don't think she minded /__/.

8. When I woke up this morning, I got dressed /__/, brushed /__/ my teeth, and combed /__/ my hair.

9. My sister filled /__/ the pitcher with water and then dropped /__/ it on the floor.

10. I'm so glad you are home; I have missed /__/ you!

Ending -ed

Name _____

Silent "E" Past

When adding the ending **-ed** to **silent-e** words (**VCe** pattern), do not spell the new word with two **e**'s in a row.

   Example: tune + ed = tun**ed**, (not tun**ee**d)

Add the suffix **-ed** to the following **silent-e** base words. Write the new words on the lines.

1. time + ____ = _____   2. like + ____ = _____

3. bike + ____ = _____   4. save + ____ = _____

5. hope + ____ = _____   6. skate + ____ = _____

7. tire + ____ = _____   8. bake + ____ = _____

9. scare + ____ = _____   10. dare + ____ = _____

Fill in each line with the word from the box that best completes the sentence.

| skated | ruled | poked | tired | raked |

11. Nelly _____ on the small lake every winter.

12. The old dog was too _____ to run fast.

13. Betsy _____ the lawn for Dad.

14. Eve _____ Ron on his shoulder.

15. The king _____ for twenty years.

Name _____

CVC and "ED"

When adding the ending **-ed** to closed-syllable words (**CVC** pattern) ending in one consonant, double the last consonant before adding **-ed.** This is true for all consonants except the letter *z.* Do not double the last consonant in base words that end in blends, digraphs, and already existing double consonants (**ff, ll, ss**).

Example: nod + **ed** = nodd**ed**

Choose the word from the box below that best completes each sentence. You will need to add **-ed** to the words when writing them on the lines. Don't forget to double the consonants.

| hug | tap | pop | jog |
| chop | rip | bat | drop |

1. My teacher _____ me on the shoulder and told me to stop talking.

2. I _____ a hole in my shirt at recess today.

3. We _____ around the gym to warm up for the game.

4. Mom _____ the celery into small pieces for the tuna salad.

5. Sammy _____ third in the baseball lineup today.

6. I _____ my baby sister and told her it would be okay.

7. When the clown _____ the balloon, it scared all of us.

8. Lisa _____ the vase of flowers, and water got all over the floor.

Ending -ed

Name _____

Three Sounds of "ED"

Add the ending **-ed** to each base word. Listen carefully to the sound at the end of the word. Then write the sound of **-ed,** /ed/, /d/, or /t/, on the line next to each word.

Example: yank + ed = yanked /t/

1. crunch + ____ = _____ /___/

2. thrill + ____ = _____ /___/

3. help + ____ = _____ /___/

4. dust + ____ = _____ /___/

5. call + ____ = _____ /___/

6. trick + ____ = _____ /___/

7. jell + ____ = _____ /___/

8. hike + ____ = _____ /___/

Now add the ending **-ed** to each base word below and write a sentence using the new word.

| bake | postpone | distract | contact |

9. _____

10. _____

11. _____

12. _____

Crossing "ED"

Match each clue with an **-ed** word from the box. Write the words in the puzzle.

blended	drilled	melted	sniffed	yelled
blinked	honked	rested	wished	

Across
2. changed from solid to liquid
5. relaxed
7. screamed
8. smelled
9. mix together

Down
1. quickly closed your eyes
3. hoped for
4. made a hole
6. made noise with a horn

Name _____

The Meaning of "ER"

The ending **-er** is added to some base words to make new words.

> Adding **-er** sometimes means more.
>
> **Example:** strong + **er** = strong**er**
>
> Sometimes adding **-er** makes reference to a person.
>
> **Example:** sing + **er** = sing**er**   bank + **er** = bank**er**

Add the ending **-er** to the following base words to make new words. Rewrite each new word on the line. Then, on the next line, write what the **-er** you added means (*more* or a *person*).

1. kind + ___ = _____   _____

2. sick + ___ = _____   _____

3. work + ___ = _____   _____

4. think + ___ = _____   _____

5. cold + ___ = _____   _____

6. paint + ___ = _____   _____

7. slow + ___ = _____   _____

8. teach + ___ = _____   _____

9. build + ___ = _____   _____

10. thick + ___ = _____   _____

Name _____

Breaking "ER" Rules

When adding the ending **-er** to a **silent-e** syllable (**VCe** pattern), only add the letter **r** because the letter **e** is already at the end of the syllable.

   Example: hike + er = hik**er** (not hik**eer**)

Add the ending **-er** to the following **silent-e** words. Then rewrite the words.

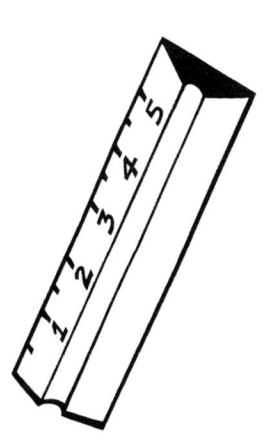

1. cute + ___ = _____

2. give + ___ = _____

3. dance + ___ = _____

4. safe + ___ = _____

5. rule + ___ = _____

Fill in each line with the **-er** word from the box that best completes the sentence.

| voter | wider | baker | skater | braver |

6. Men in the military must be a lot _____ than I am.

7. When I turn 18, I will register to be a _____.

8. My mom is a great _____; everyone loves her chocolate-chip cookies.

9. When I grow up, I want to be a professional ice _____.

10. Our car is _____ than that narrow road.

Ending -er

Daily Skill-Builders Spelling & Phonics 4–5
walch.com © 2004 Walch Publishing

103

Name _____

Adding "ER" to "Y"

When adding the ending **-er** to words that end in **y**, change the **y** to **i**, and then add **-er**.

Example: lazy + er = laz**i**er
The **y** is gone, and now there is an **i** in its place.

Add **-er** to the following words. Be sure to use the correct spelling.

1. scary + er = _____
2. hairy + er = _____
3. tiny + er = _____
4. tidy + er = _____
5. happy + er = _____
6. silly + er = _____
7. pretty + er = _____
8. funny + er = _____

Use four of your answers from above in sentences of your own.

9. _____
10. _____
11. _____
12. _____

Name _____

"ER" and CVC Words

When a word ends with one vowel followed by one consonant, double the consonant before adding **-er**.

   Example: thin + er = thinner

Add **-er** to the following words. Do not forget to double the consonants.

1. slim + er = _____   2. bat + er = _____

3. hot + er = _____   4. run + er = _____

5. big + er = _____   6. chat + er = _____

Read each sentence and the word below the line. Add **-er** to the word to complete the sentence. Write the new word on the line.

7. It seems the more I eat, the _____ I get.
                                    fat

8. I waved to the ____ _____ on the street.
                      jog

9. My little brother is _____ than he was a few minutes ago
                            sad
   because he lost his toy.

10. The grass over there is _____ than the grass on the hill.
                                flat

11. My dad thinks I am a really good gift _____.
                                            wrap

Ending -er

What Does "EST" Mean?

The ending **-er** means *more*. The ending **-est** means *most*.

Examples: Strong**er** means *more strong*. Strong**est** means *most strong*.

Read the sentences and the **-er** and **-est** words below. Circle the word that best completes each sentence.

1. My car is (faster, fastest) than your car.

2. I am the (taller, tallest) student in my class.

3. I am (older, oldest) than all of my cousins.

4. Shawn is the (quicker, quickest) player on our soccer team.

5. I think that today is the (colder, coldest) day of the year.

6. Today seems a lot (longer, longest) than yesterday.

7. This lake is (deeper, deepest) than the one I went swimming in last week.

8. I can see the (higher, highest) point on that mountain.

9. The crust on that pizza is the (thicker, thickest) I have ever seen!

10. My piece of pie is much (smaller, smallest) than your piece.

Name _____

Breaking "EST" Rules

When adding the ending -est to a **silent-e** syllable (VCe pattern), only add the letters **st** because the letter **e** is already at the end of the syllable.

   Example: safe + est = saf**est** (not saf**eest**)

Add the ending -est to the following **silent-e** words. Then write the new word on the line. Read the new words as you write them.

1. safe + ___ = _____

2. brave + ___ = _____

3. wide + ___ = _____

4. close + ___ = _____

5. nice + ___ = _____

Fill in each line with the word from the box that best completes the sentence.

| cutest | latest | whitest | rudest | purest |

6. Have you heard the _____ news about the hikers rescued in the mountains?

7. That is the _____ baby I have ever seen.

8. My mother has the _____ teeth of anyone I know.

9. I think that the _____ water comes from that spring over there.

10. Regrettably, the captain of the soccer team displayed the _____ behavior on the team.

Ending -est

Name _____

Searching for More and Most

In the word search, circle the **-er** or **-est** form of the words that are listed in the box. Words can be found vertically, horizontally, diagonally, or backwards.

bold	brave	joke
lazy	shop	strong
thick	weld	wild

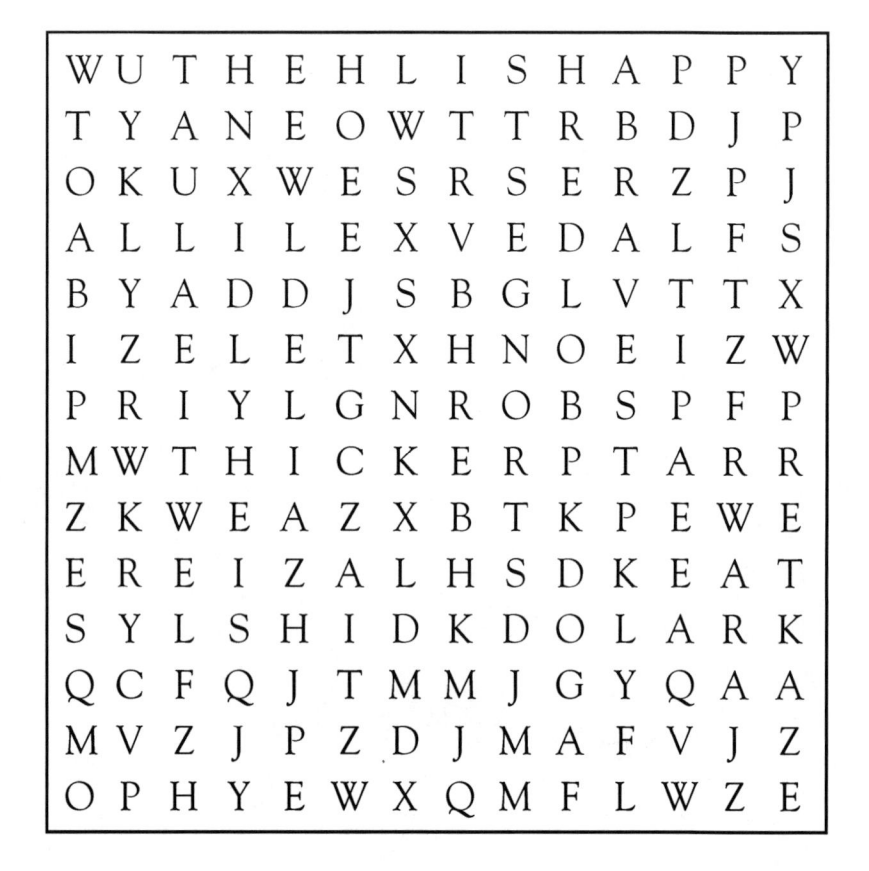

```
W U T H E H L I S H A P P Y
T Y A N E O W T T R B D J P
O K U X W E S R S E R Z P J
A L L I L E X V E D A L F S
B Y A D D J S B G L V T T X
I Z E L E T X H N O E I Z W
P R I Y L G N R O B S P F P
M W T H I C K E R P T A R R
Z K W E A Z X B T K P E W E
E R E I Z A L H S D K E A T
S Y L S H I D K D O L A R K
Q C F Q J T M M J G Y Q A A
M V Z J P Z D J M A F V J Z
O P H Y E W X Q M F L W Z E
```

Endings -er and -est

Name _____

Prefix Power

A **prefix** is a letter or group of letters added to the beginning of a word to change the meaning. The prefixes **un-** and **dis-** both mean *not* or *the opposite of*.

> **Examples:** un + lock = **un**lock (*the opposite of lock*)
> dis + like = **dis**like (*not like*)

Choose the word from the box below that best completes each sentence. Add the prefix **un-** to each word before writing it on the line.

> fair   load   safe   happy   pack

1. I feel _____ when I don't wear my seatbelt in the car.

2. Please _____ the dishwasher and put the dishes away.

3. That punishment seems _____ for such a minor offense.

4. That crying baby must be _____ about something.

5. You need to _____ you suitcase when we get home.

Write a sentence using each **dis-** word below.

6. disobey _____
7. disagree _____
8. disappear _____
9. discomfort _____
10. disconnect _____

Prefixes *un-* and *dis-*

Daily Skill-Builders Spelling & Phonics 4–5
walch.com © 2004 Walch Publishing

Name _____

Before and Again

The prefix **pre-** means *before*. The prefix **re-** means *again*.

Examples: **pre** + view = **pre**view (*view before*)
re + heat = **re**heat (*heat again*)

Read the definitions below. Write the **pre-** or **re-** word next to the definition.

1. to fill again _____
2. to heat before _____
3. to read again _____
4. to write again _____
5. to pay before _____
6. to play again _____
7. before game _____
8. before school _____

Fill in each line with the word from above that best completes the sentence.

9. Please _____ the oven so I can cook dinner.

10. I liked that book so much that I think I will _____ it.

11. Will they _____ my favorite show if I miss it?

12. I went to _____ the year before I started kindergarten.

13. My glass is empty. Will you _____ it?

14. How long will the _____ show be on before they actually start playing?

15. I don't like the draft of my story, so I am going to _____ it.

16. My dad likes to _____ his bills so he has enough money.

Name _____

Prefixes Again

The prefix **mis-** means *badly, wrongly,* or *opposite of*. The prefix **non-** means *not, without,* or *opposite of*.

>   **Examples:** mis + treat = **mis**treat (*treat badly*)
>   non + living = **non**living (*not living*)

Read the clues below. Add **mis-** or **non-** to the underlined word, and write it on the line.

1. The yogurt I had for breakfast had no <u>fat</u> in it. It was _____ yogurt.

2. People always <u>spell</u> my first name incorrectly. I hate when they _____ it.

3. I thought I <u>understood</u> the directions. When I got my paper back, I realized I _____ them.

4. I like to read <u>fiction</u> books. I think they are much more interesting than _____ books.

5. My brother and I usually <u>behave</u> for our babysitter, but sometimes we _____.

6. I found where I <u>placed</u> my glasses. I thought I had _____ them.

7. The plane does not <u>stop</u> between Boston and Atlanta. It is a _____ flight.

8. Your story does not make any <u>sense</u>. It is complete _____!

Name _____

Is That Too Much?

The prefix **over-** means *too much*. The prefix **im-** means *not*.

Examples: over + pay = **over**pay (*pay too much*)
im + possible = **im**possible (*not possible*)

Read each sentence below. Write **over-** or **im-** on the line to complete the word and have the sentence make sense.

1. Put only a little bit of food out for the cat, or else she will _____eat.

2. Don't be _____patient. Good things come to those who wait.

3. The cashier _____charged my brother for his jeans. I know they were on sale.

4. If you leave soup on the stove too long, it will _____heat.

5. It is _____proper to walk out in the middle of a person's speech.

6. Make sure you don't _____sleep in the morning. We need to leave on time.

Add **over-** or **im-** to each word below. Then write the definition of each word on the line.

7. _____eat _____

8. _____patient _____

9. _____charged _____

10. _____heat _____

Prefixes Across and Down

Match each clue with a word from the box. Write the words in the puzzle.

nonstop	preview	reread	disagree	impossible
oversleep	refill	unlock	impatient	misbehave

Across
1. to not agree
4. behave badly
6. without stopping
8. to fill again
9. not patient
10. the opposite of lock

Down
2. to read again
3. to view before
5. not possible
7. to sleep too much

Prefix Review

Name _____

What Does "LESS" Mean?

The suffix **-less** means *none* or *without*.

Example: use + less = use**less** (*no use for*)

Read the following definitions. Write the suffixed word on the line.

1. no mind   _____
2. without rest   _____
3. without help   _____
4. no hope   _____
5. without bone   _____
6. no spine   _____
7. without life   _____
8. without home   _____
9. no name   _____
10. without wire   _____

Fill in each line with the word from the box that best completes the sentence.

useless	restless	helpless	homeless	boneless

11. I want _____ chicken and potatoes for dinner.
12. The _____ puppy was _____ until we adopted it.
13. Ted could not sit still because he was _____.
14. At birth, a kitten is _____ without its mother.
15. A broken lamp is _____.

Daily Skill-Builders Spelling & Phonics 4–5
walch.com © 2004 Walch Publishing

Suffix -less

What Does "FUL" Mean?

The suffix **-ful** means *full of*. The suffix **-ful** is always spelled with only one l.

Example: use + ful = use**ful** (means *full of use* or *able to be used*)

Add the suffix **-ful** to the following base words. Then write the meaning of each **-ful** word on the second line.

1. help _____ _____
2. hope _____ _____
3. thank _____ _____
4. care _____ _____
5. respect _____ _____
6. pain _____ _____

Fill in each line with the word from above that best completes the sentence.

7. When I fell off my bike, it was very _____.

8. Now I know I will be more _____ when riding my bike.

9. My brother was _____ because he carried me back to our house.

10. My brother was also _____ because he didn't make fun of me for falling off my bike.

11. I am _____ that I didn't get hurt worse.

12. I am _____ that it will not happen again.

Suffix -ful

Name _____

Finding "LESS" and "FUL"

In the word search, circle a suffixed form of each word listed in the box. Words can be found vertically, horizontally, diagonally, or backwards.

bone	care	hand
help	hope	life
rest	thank	wire

```
I Q W H N E C R T P Z M U I
P X D J J X Q M S L G R H O
H W S H Z D J S X U I W Z G
B C Q S N K E F H F B K R N
M B A U E L P A Z K U V H D
C X E R E L N W B N U T O P
P N S F E D T O C A S H P A
H O I W F F N S T H G R E Q
Y L C U Q E U T E T T K F K
A N L J L E A L F R N Q U L
B D I E W I R E L E S S L P
N S S E L P L E H U P N D D
U S E B E V K R X F P J O V
I B G E Q Z P M A I B W L F
```

Suffixes -less and -ful

Name _____

It Ends with "Y"

The suffix **-y** makes a word that describes. The suffix **-ly** makes a word that tells how something is done.

    Examples: rusty   loudly

Add **-y** or **-ly** to the base words below. Write the suffix on the first line, then write the new word on the second line.

1. luck + _____ = _____
2. lone + _____ = _____
3. hand + _____ = _____
4. late + _____ = _____
5. mess + _____ = _____
6. love + _____ = _____
7. quick + _____ = _____

Fill in each line with the word from above that best completes the sentence.

8. Were you _____ enough to get tickets for the concert?

9. Your desk is _____ and needs to be cleaned.

10. That dress looks _____ on you.

11. Walk _____ because we are late.

Suffixes -y and -ly

Why Suffixes?

Match each clue with a word from the box. Write the words in the puzzle.

| handy | lonely | lucky | puffy | safely |
| lively | lovely | messy | quickly | |

Across
1. fast
3. helpful or useful
5. beautiful
6. without harm
8. good fortune

Down
2. feeling alone
4. not neat
5. lots of energy
7. big or swollen

Name _____

"TION"

The suffix **-tion** makes the /shŭn/ sound. When added to a base word it changes an action word to a word that names something.

Add the suffix **-tion** to the following base words. Then write the new word, along with its definition.

1. prevent _____

2. relax _____

3. locate _____

4. construct _____

5. dictate _____

6. produce _____

7. infect _____

8. direct _____

Use two **-tion** words from above in sentences of your own.

9. _____

10. _____

Suffix *-tion*

Making "TION" Words

Read the definitions of the **-tion** words on the left. Then put the syllables in the boxes in the correct order to make **-tion** words. The first one has been done for you.

#	Definition	Syllables	Answer
1.	the making of a gift to charity	tion / do / na	donation
2.	a letter or note inviting you to a party	ta / vi / tion / in	_____
3.	a relaxing time away from school or work	ca / va / tion	_____
4.	adding numbers together to get a sum	i / tion / add	_____
5.	the answer	lu / so / tion	_____
6.	the act or process of learning	tion / ca / ed / u	_____
7.	the act of telling the future	dic / pre / tion	_____
8.	the act or process of making something new	ven / tion / in	_____

120

Daily Skill-Builders Spelling & Phonics 4–5
walch.com © 2004 Walch Publishing

Suffix *-tion*

Another "ION" Suffix

The suffix **-sion** makes either the /shŭn/ sound as in *mansion* or the /zhŭn/ sound as in *vision*.

Read the following words, and underline the **-sion** in each one. Then write the sound it makes after each word.

Examples: mansion /shun/   vision /zhun/

1. television /_____/
2. decision /_____/
3. invasion /_____/
4. division /_____/
5. explosion /_____/
6. confusion /_____/
7. tension /_____/
8. suspension /_____/
9. conclusion /_____/
10. erosion /_____/
11. extension /_____/
12. expansion /_____/

Fill in each line with the word from the box that best completes the sentence.

| division | invasion | mansion | television | explosion | decision |

13. Randy lives in a huge _____ in the city.

14. Before bedtime, Susan likes to watch _____.

15. The loud _____ shook the ground.

16. There was an _____ of ants in the kitchen.

17. In math, Nancy can do long _____ very well.

18. I can't make a _____ about what I want to eat for dinner.

"TION" or "SION"?

Match each clue with a word from the box. Write the words in the puzzle.

| conclusion | donation | invention | solution | vacation |
| division | fiction | location | television | |

Across
1. used for entertainment or information
5. a break from work or school
6. a story that is not true
8. an answer to a problem
9. where a place is

Down
2. something newly created
3. something final, the end
4. opposite of multiplication
7. money or items given away

Name_____

"ANCE" or "ENCE"?

The suffixes **-ance** and **-ence** can be difficult because the **a** and the **e** are easily confused. Both **-ance** and **-ence** mean *act* or *state of being*.

> Add **-ance** when a word comes before it.
>   **Example:** perform + ance = perform**ance**
>   *Perform* is a word, so it takes the **-ance** ending.
> Add **-ence** when a word part comes before it.
>   **Example:** sci + ence = sci**ence**
>   *Sci* is a word part.

Add the suffixes **-ance** or **-ence** to make words below. Use the rules in the box above to help you. Then write the definition of the word using the meaning of the suffix.

1. attend_____
   _____

2. audi_____
   _____

3. clear_____
   _____

4. sil_____
   _____

5. intellig_____
   _____

6. accept_____
   _____

"ANCE" and "ENCE" Sentences

Add the correct suffix to each word below. Then choose the word that best completes each sentence.

attend_____	allow_____	assist_____	sil_____
confid_____	audi_____	perform_____	sci_____
appear_____	viol_____		

1. My favorite subject in school is _____ because we do experiments.

2. Please wait to clap until the end of the singer's _____.

3. I didn't miss a day of school this year, so I have perfect _____.

4. The actor froze when he looked out at the _____.

5. I get an _____ every week if I do all my chores.

6. I won't watch that movie—it has too much _____ in it.

7. Ask the librarian for _____ if you can't find the book.

8. My teacher asks for _____ when we are taking a test.

9. The more I practice playing my flute, the more _____ I will have to play in public.

10. My dad could tell by my _____ that I just woke up.

Name _____

Wrap It Up!

Create new words by adding suffixes and endings from the box below. There may be more than one choice for some words. Try to use each suffix or ending only once. Then use the word in a sentence.

| -s | -es | -er | -est | -y | -ly | -ty | -ing | -less | -ful | -ed |

1. box____ = _____
   _____

2. mess____ = _____
   _____

3. thank____ = _____
   _____

4. swing____ = _____
   _____

5. wire____ = _____
   _____

6. strong____ = _____
   _____

7. hug____ = _____
   _____

8. lone____ = _____
   _____

9. six____ = _____
   _____

10. quick____ = _____
    _____

Suffix and Ending Review

That Controlling "R"!

When a vowel is followed by the letter **r**, the vowel is neither short nor long. It is controlled by the letter **r**. Use the key words in the box to help you remember the sounds of **r**-controlled vowels.

| **ar** as in *car* | **er** as in *fern* | **ir** as in *bird* |
| **or** as in *horn* | **ur** as in *burn* | |

Circle the words with **r**-controlled vowels in the sentences below. Then, on the line at the end of the sentence, write another word you can think of with the same **r**-controlled vowel.

1. I love to look at the stars at night. _____

2. Owen is too short to go on that ride. _____

3. My class took a field trip to the circus. _____

4. I always burp when I drink soda. _____

5. On the weekends I go shopping with my mother. _____

6. I want to be an artist when I grow up. _____

7. The corn will ripen by late August. _____

8. The nurse wrapped my knee in a bandage after I fell. _____

9. Pepper makes me sneeze. _____

10. My aunt is going to be thirty next week. _____

Name _____

Picturing "AR"

Write the name of the picture on the lines.

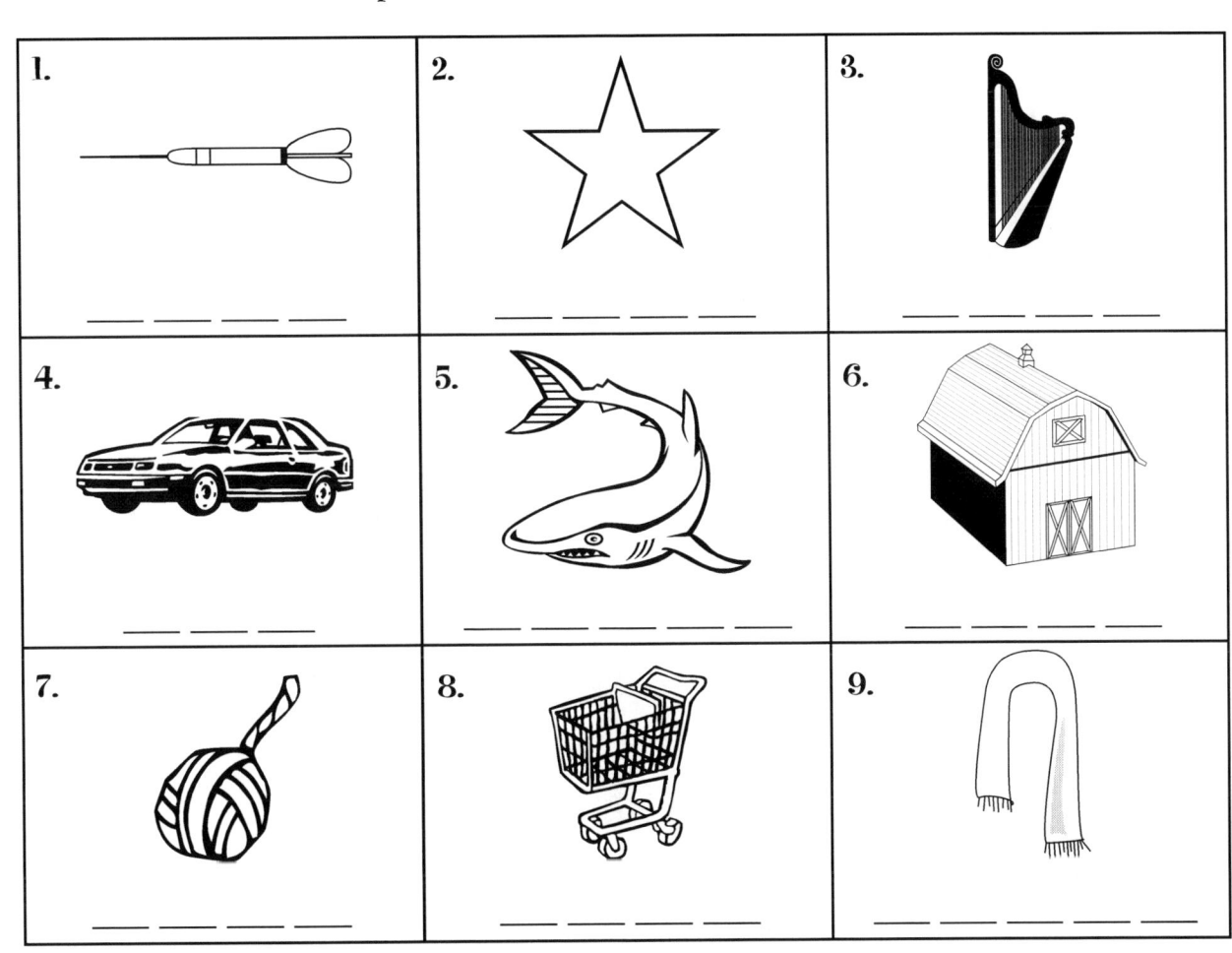

1.	2.	3.
4.	5.	6.
7.	8.	9.

Use the following two-syllable **ar** words in sentences of your own.

garden   garlic   harvest

10. _____

11. _____

12. _____

R-Controlled Vowels—*ar*

Name _____

Picturing "OR"

Write the name of the picture on the lines.

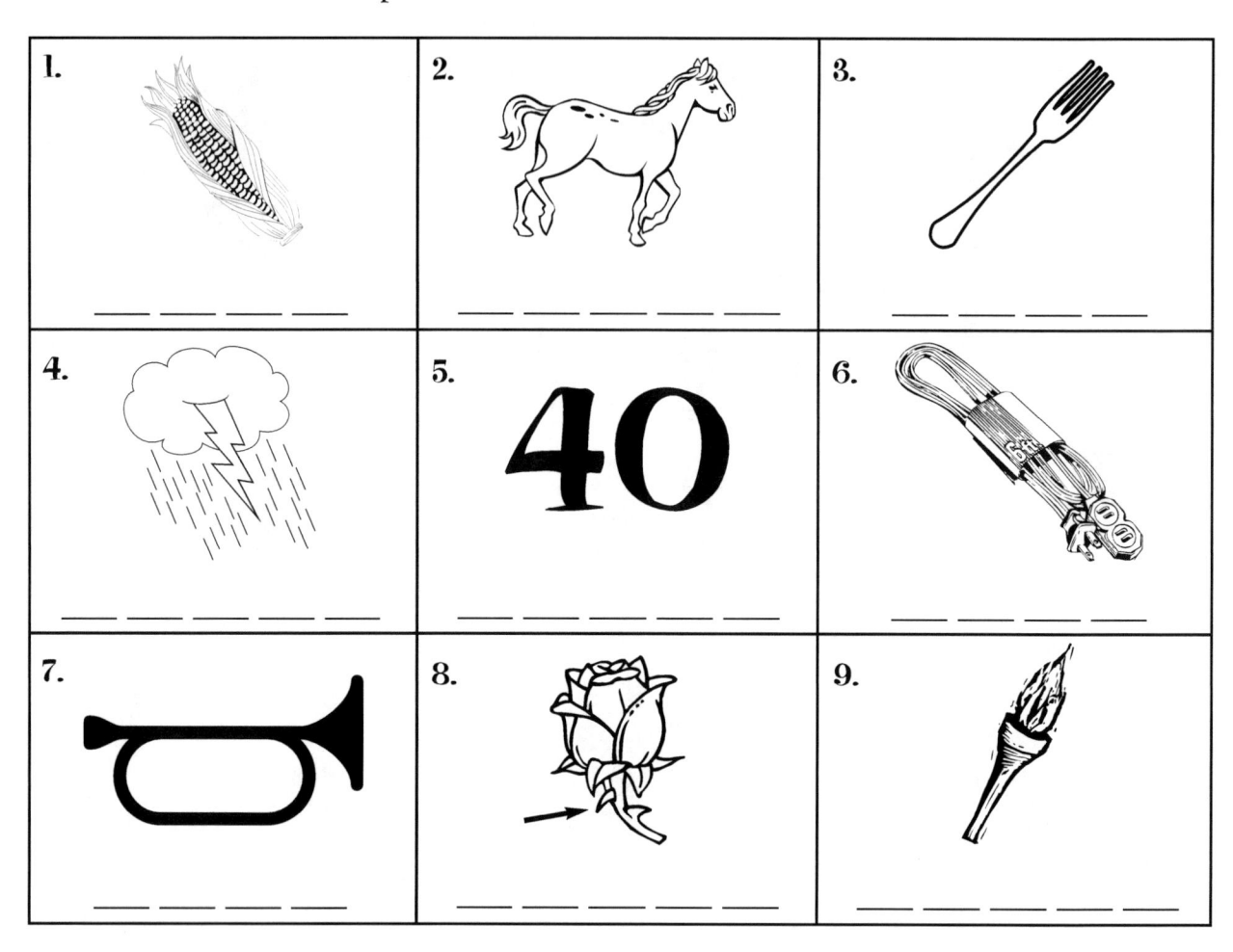

1. (corn)	2. (horse)	3. (fork)
_ _ _ _	_ _ _ _ _	_ _ _ _
4. (storm)	5. 40	6. (cord)
_ _ _ _ _	_ _ _ _	_ _ _ _
7. (horn)	8. (thorn)	9. (torch)
_ _ _ _	_ _ _ _ _	_ _ _ _ _

Use three of the words from above in sentences of your own.

10. _____

11. _____

12. _____

128 Daily Skill-Builders Spelling & Phonics 4–5
walch.com © 2004 Walch Publishing

R-Controlled Vowels—or

Name _____

"AR" and "OR" Rulebreakers

Sometimes **ar** can sound like /er/ as in the word *calendar*. It often sounds like /er/ when it comes at the end of a word with more than one syllable. The **ar** can also sound like /or/ as in the word *warm*. This sound is usually found in one-syllable words.

Sometimes **or** can sound like /er/ as in the word *doctor*, especially at the end of a word with more than one syllable.

Add **ar** or **or** to complete the words below. After each word, write the sound you hear in the **r**-controlled syllable.

1. doll____ /___/
2. harb____ /___/
3. tract____ /___/
4. regul____ /___/
5. mot____ /___/
6. fav____ /___/
7. simil____ /___/
8. liz____d /___/
9. act____ /___/
10. invent____ /___/
11. forw____d /___/
12. cell____ /___/
13. janit____ /___/
14. wiz____d /___/
15. must____d /___/
16. raz____ /___/

Now use four of the words from above in sentences of your own.

17. _____
18. _____
19. _____
20. _____

R-Controlled Vowels—*ar* and *or*

Name _____

"ER" Sound

Most words with the /er/ sound are spelled with the **er** combination, but it is a good idea to use a dictionary as a reference when you are not sure which **r**-syllable combination to use in spelling these types of words.

Add the following **r**-syllable combinations to the sounds below.

1. er   **2. ir**   **3. ur**

h____   st____   bl____

monst____   f____   f____

bank____   s____   sp____

stick____   d____t   c____l

sist____   fl____t   h____t

hamst____   b____th   c____b

Use two words from each column above in sentences of your own.

4. _____

5. _____

6. _____

7. _____

8. _____

9. _____

Name _____

"ER," "IR," or "UR"?

All words below have the /er/ sound. Complete each word with the correct r-syllable spelling. The choices are **er**, **ir**, and **ur**.

1. broth____   memb____   g____l

2. silv____   sunb____n   s____vive

3. moth____   d____ty   ret____n

4. dist____b   v____b   sw____l

5. b____th   sh____t   b____st

6. occ____   ch____p   l____k

7. bak____y   thund____   b____p

8. t____mite   summ____   numb____

9. h____   ch____ch   squ____m

10. hamst____   f____n   G____many

R-Controlled Vowels—*er, ir,* and *ur*

Daily Skill-Builders Spelling & Phonics 4–5
walch.com © 2004 Walch Publishing

131

Name _____

You're in Control!

Read the following words with **r**-controlled vowels. Circle the **r** and the vowel it goes with in each word. The first one has been done for you.

1. chapt(er)   garden   lord   tornado
2. hornet   brother sister   father
3. doctor   worn   quart   dwarf
4. curl   proper   squirm   curb
5. winter   pitcher hurt   scarf

Fill in each line with the word from the box that best completes the sentence. Some words will not be used.

boring	short	morning	survive	forty
energy	first	expert	person	cartoons

6. I always have a lot of _____ when I wake up in the _____.

7. I am always the _____ one awake in our house.

8. My mom always tells me that I am a morning _____.

9. One time I was awake for an hour and _____ minutes before anyone else woke up.

10. It was _____ all by myself, so I turned on the television and watched _____.

Daily Skill-Builders Spelling & Phonics 4–5
walch.com © 2004 Walch Publishing

R-Controlled Vowels—*ar, or, er, ir,* and *ur*

Name _____

R-Controlled Clues

Fill in each line with the word from the box that best matches the clue.

| barks | slippers | turkey | morning | circle | garden |
| fork | birthday | cartoon | teacher | picture | hornet |

1. a round shape _____

2. a bird on a farm or in the wild _____

3. what a dog does _____

4. what you might watch on television _____

5. where you would plant vegetables or flowers _____

6. what you might wear on your feet to keep them warm _____

7. when you were born _____

8. You could get stung by a _____.

9. You eat steak with a knife and a _____.

10. when you usually wake up _____

11. Smile so I can take a _____.

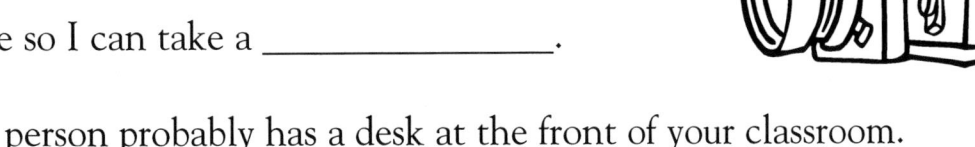

12. This person probably has a desk at the front of your classroom. _____

R-Controlled Vowels—*ar, or, er, ir,* and *ur*

Controlling Crossword

Match each clue with a word from the box. Write the words in the puzzle.

barn	firm	star	hamster	foghorn
blur	sir	verb	hornet	hurricane

Across
2. not clear
4. what is sounded to give ships a warning
6. a rodent with large cheeks and a short tail
8. a wasp that can sting

Down
1. a word expressing action
2. a place for keeping farm animals
3. can be seen in the night sky
4. hard
5. a tropical cyclone
7. another name for a man

Name _____

"AY" Sentences

The letters **ay** are considered a vowel digraph because the **a** and the **y** make one sound. They make the sound of long a /ā/.

Fill in each line with the word from the box that best completes the sentence.

| play | hay | way | jay | gray |
| clay | ray | stray | delay | runway |

1. Which _____ did the snake go?

2. The blue _____ is my favorite bird.

3. Mary likes to make crafts with _____.

4. I hope the slow train will not _____ my trip.

5. Did you see the _____ of sunshine through the clouds?

6. Bill found a _____ cat and took it home.

7. Please do not _____ in the street.

8. The horses ate all the _____ on the farm.

9. When you mix black and white together, you get _____.

Vowel Digraph *ay*

Name _____

Another Long "A" Digraph

The letters **ai** have the long **a** /ā/ sound. This vowel digraph is often found in the middle of a word with a long **a** sound before one or more consonants.

Read the sentences below. Circle the **ai** words that have the long **a** /ā/ sound. Then, at the end of the sentence, write another word with the same sound as the word you circled.

1. My favorite thing to do in art class is to paint pictures.
   _____

2. My dog always wags its tail when I get home from school.
   _____

3. I don't want it to rain because our game will be canceled.
   _____

4. Please wait to cross the road until you are sure no cars are coming.
   _____

5. You won't get paid for your chores until the end of the week.
   _____

6. When I grow up, I want to sail around the world. _____

7. There is a stain on the rug from where you spilled the juice.
   _____

8. I am worried that I will fail my math test today. _____

Name _____

Picturing "AI" and "EI"

The letters **ai** and **ei** have the long a /ā/ sound. Write **ai** or **ei** words on the lines to name the pictures.

1.	2.	3.
_____	_____	_____
4.	5.	6.
_____	_____	_____

Think of two **ai** words and two **ei** words and use them in sentences below.

7. _____

8. _____

9. _____

10. _____

Vowel Digraphs ai and ei

Name _____

"AY" or "AI"?

Match each clue with a word from the box. Write the words in the puzzle.

| afraid | decay | remain | stain | sway |
| birthday | painter | snail | stray | |

Across
2. the day a person is born
4. to stay
6. to wander or roam
8. to rot

Down
1. someone who paints
3. to ruin by spotting
5. to be scared
6. an animal that lives in a spiral protective shell
7. to move from side to side

Vowel Digraphs *ay* and *ai*

Name _____

Long "A" Search

The letters **ay** are considered a vowel digraph because the **a** and the **y** make one sound. They make the sound of long **a** /ā/.

In the word search below, circle only the words from the box that have the long **a** sound. Words can be found horizontally, vertically, diagonally, and backwards.

tarp	sprain	cans	stay	cane
birthday	weigh	chart	chain	daisy
baker	hay	biker	walks	sleigh

```
H S C A T P E G K I K L A T
B L M J R H N I A R P S O G
I N A E S W A T C W A L K S
R B C A N E J M B L G F I A
T I H C F I P A O S N T A H
H O A D O G G U T S H D U T
D F T G I H B A M D A K J P
A L K S Y E Y N A F Y L M N
Y R R S A H C P A O C A E G
G B I N L F D I P B I B D I
M A M K S E E A P C H A I N
D T U C J H I R L I F K E J
U V C A M P L G E N H E D A
P A R T S V B U H W C R O L
```

Vowel Digraphs *ay*, *ai*, and *ei*

Name _____

"EY" at the End

The letters **ey** usually say the long **e** /ē/ sound as in the word *key*. Often when the long **e** sound comes at the end of a word or syllable, it is spelled with **ey**. There are no consonants after it.

Match the words with the definitions below. Write the letter of the correct definition on the line.

_____ 1. hockey   **a.** a grain

_____ 2. jersey   **b.** a sport

_____ 3. valley   **c.** a large bird

_____ 4. chimney   **d.** a shirt

_____ 5. barley   **e.** a place that smoke comes out of

_____ 6. kidney   **f.** a body part; an organ

_____ 7. turkey   **g.** a green plant

_____ 8. parsley   **h.** lowland between mountains

Sometimes the letters **ey** stand for the long **a** sound. Read the words below. Write the **ey** words in the correct column.

monkey	survey	obey	barley
they	kidney	Shirley	Grey

9.   Sounds like a   10.   Sounds like e

_____   _____

_____   _____

_____   _____

_____   _____

Name _____

The Sounds of "EA"

The letters **ea** can make three different sounds.

> The letters **ea** can make the long e /ē/ sound.
>   **Example:** meat
>
> The letters **ea** can make the short e /ĕ/ sound.
>   **Example:** bread
>
> The letters **ea** can make the long a /ā/ sound.
>   **Example:** steak

On the lines, write the sound the **ea** makes in the words below. The first one has been done for you.

1. heat /ē/
2. break _____
3. sweat _____
4. thread _____

5. sea _____
6. beach _____
7. great _____
8. dream _____

9. head _____
10. stream _____
11. breath _____
12. please _____

Use three words from above in sentences of your own. Use one word that has the long **e** sound, one word with the long **a** sound, and one word with the short **e** sound.

13. _____

14. _____

15. _____

Vowel Digraph ea

Name _____

More on "EA"

Use only the **ea** words in the box that make the long **e** sound to complete the sentences below.

| speak | dream | great | teach | sweat | seal |

1. We saw a _____ on our field trip to the aquarium.

2. Will you _____ me how to play that song on the piano?

3. My _____ was so scary last night that it woke me up.

4. Only _____ when you raise your hand and are called upon.

Use only the **ea** words in the box that make the short **e** sound to complete the sentences below.

| stream | bread | steak | spread | sweat | beach |

5. What kind of _____ do you want when I make your toast?

6. Do you want me to _____ butter or jelly on your toast?

7. We ran around the gym so many times that I started to _____.

Use only the **ea** words in the box that make the long **a** sound to complete the sentences below.

| meat | thread | seat | great | team | break |

8. You have been working for a while, so you can take a _____.

9. Her performance was so _____ that everyone cheered.

Name _____

Long "E"

The letters **ee, ea,** and **ey** can all stand for the long e /ē/ sound.

Examples: bee   bean   key

Fill in each line with the word from the box that best completes the sentence.

| green | cream | monkey | agree | deep | clean |
| hockey | easy | meal | cheese | money | week |

1. Do you have enough lunch _____ for today?

2. I always eat a bowl of ice _____ after dinner.

3. My favorite sport to play is ice _____.

4. You can't watch the movie until you _____ your room.

5. I am so excited that we have next _____ off from school.

6. Look at that _____ hanging from the tree.

7. My dad packed me a ham and _____ sandwich for lunch today.

8. I can't wait until spring when the grass is _____ again.

9. Our math homework is so _____ that it will only take me a few minutes to do it.

10. Do you _____ that we should wait until it stops raining to go fishing?

11. How _____ is the lake right here at this spot?

12. My favorite _____ of the day is breakfast.

Vowel Digraphs *ee, ea,* and *ey*

Name _____

Which Is Correct?

The following words with the letters **ee** and **ea** have the **long e** /ē/ sound. Only one word in each pair is spelled correctly. Circle the correct spelling in each pair.

1.	teeth	teath	2.	sheet	sheat
3.	frea	free	4.	neat	neet
5.	steam	steem	6.	bleed	blead
7.	meel	meal	8.	green	grean
9.	beem	beam	10.	leef	leaf
11.	street	streat	12.	sheep	sheap
13.	easy	eesy	14.	keep	keap
15.	treat	treet	16.	speak	speek

Now write the correct spelling of each word in the correct column below.

17.   ee   18.   ea

_____   _____
_____   _____
_____   _____
_____   _____
_____   _____
_____   _____
_____   _____
_____   _____

Name _____

Sound Alikes

Some words that sound alike have two different spellings, depending on their meanings. These words are called **homophones.** Look at the spellings and meanings of the following homophones.

see—to look	sea—a large body of water
meet—come together	meat—food from an animal
week—days	weak—not strong
seem—appears to be	seam—a line where things are joined
creek—a small stream	creak—squeaking sound
tee—a small peg used in golf	tea—a hot drink
flee—to leave quickly	flea—a small insect or parasite
beet—a vegetable	beat—to hit or pound
steel—made of iron and carbon	steal—to take another's property
peek—to look quickly	peak—a pointed end or top

Circle the word that best fits the meaning in each sentence.

1. I cannot (see, sea) through this fog.

2. There are seven days in a (weak, week).

3. Bacon is my favorite (meet, meat).

4. Bob will climb to the mountain's (peek, peak).

5. I like to drink hot (tea, tee) after dinner.

6. Jade ripped the (seem, seam) on her dress.

7. There is a (creek, creak) that runs through my yard.

8. The small (flee, flea) can jump very high.

Vowel Digraphs *ee* and *ea*

Daily Skill-Builders Spelling & Phonics 4–5
walch.com © 2004 Walch Publishing

145

Long "E" Crossing

Match each clue with a word from the box. Write the words in the puzzle.

| beam | clean | eel | meet | peace | street |
| chimney | creek | leash | monkey | seedling | |

Across
3. a stream of water smaller than a river
4. freedom from war
6. an ape
7. a long snakelike fish
9. a place for smoke to escape

Down
1. a road
2. a long piece of wood or metal
3. not dirty
5. a young plant
6. to come together
8. used for walking a dog

Name _____

Two Sounds for "IE"

The letters **ie** can stand for long i /ī/ as in *tie*. The letters **ie** can also stand for long e /ē/ as in *chief*.

Look at the **ie** words in the box. If a word has a long i sound, write it in the **Long i** column. If a word has a long e sound, write it in the **Long e** column.

| lie | movie | die | dried |
| pie | field | believe | married |

1. **Long i**

_____

_____

_____

_____

2. **Long e**

_____

_____

_____

_____

Fill in each line with the word from above that best completes the sentence.

3. Let's rent a _____ for you to watch on Friday.

4. That plant will _____ if you don't water it.

5. How old were your parents when they got _____?

6. Please tell me the truth; you shouldn't _____.

7. I had to wait to go out in the cold until my hair _____.

8. Wow! You ate that whole _____ by yourself!

9. There are always wild turkeys out in that _____ over there.

10. You have to see it to _____ it.

Vowel Digraph ie

Name _____

Long "E" or Long "A"?

The letters **ei** can make the long e /ē/ sound or the long a /ā/ sound.

　　Examples: protein /ē/　　veil /ā/

Circle the **ei** in each word below, and write the sound it makes after each word.

1. ceiling /___/
2. beige /___/
3. caffeine /___/
4. vein /___/
5. neither /___/
6. unveil /___/
7. receive /___/
8. sheik /___/
9. neither /___/
10. either /___/
11. protein /___/
12. reindeer /___/

Fill in each line with the word from the box that best completes the sentence.

| caffeine | veil | ceiling | receive | beige | protein |

13. The _____ fan keeps me cool at night.

14. Meat and nuts are high in _____.

15. Bernie wears his _____ coat in the rain.

16. The winner will _____ a medal.

17. The bride's _____ covered her face.

18. Don't have _____ at night; it will keep you awake.

Name _____

Two Vowels—One Sound

The letters **oa, oe,** and **ow** often make the long o /ō/ sound.

Complete each word below by writing **oa, oe,** or **ow** on the line.

1. gr_____
2. t_____s
3. c_____ch
4. thr_____t
5. b_____l
6. d_____
7. h_____
8. t_____st
9. sl_____

Fill in each line with the word from the box that best completes the sentence. Some words will not be used.

| bowl | narrow | tiptoed | throat | toe |
| road | oatmeal | toast | slowly | swallow |

10. I have a _____ of _____ every morning for breakfast.

11. My brother always eats _____ with peanut butter.

12. This morning my _____ hurts, and it's hard for me to _____ .

13. I'm eating my breakfast very _____.

14. My brother _____ across the kitchen floor to sneak another spoonful of peanut butter.

15. We're late for school, so it's time to hit the _____.

Vowel Digraphs oa, oe, and *ow*

Name _____

"OA" Sentences

Fill in each line with the **oa** word from the box that best completes the sentence. **Remember:** Say the long o /ō/ sound when reading these words.

| coaster | boat | roast | soaking | goal | coach |
| coal | toad | cockroach | toaster | goat | throat |

1. There was a _____ hopping in the _____.

2. Bradley uses _____ in his stove to keep warm.

3. Please put two slices of bread in the _____.

4. Shirley's _____ was proud of her soccer _____.

5. On the farm, Joe has three cows, two pigs, and one _____.

6. My bathing suit was _____ wet.

7. The roller _____ is lots of fun.

8. Mom will _____ a turkey for Thanksgiving.

9. I didn't go to school today because I have a sore _____.

10. Mom found a _____ in her motel room.

Name _____

"OW" and Long "O"

The letters **ow** have two sounds. They can have the **long o** /ō/ sound as in the word *show*, or the /ou/ sound as in the word *plow*.

Write **ow** on the lines to make words. Then write the sound each word makes.

Example: show /ō/

1. l_____ /__/   b_____ /__/   kn_____ /__/   sn_____ /__/
2. m_____ /__/   bl_____ /__/   cr_____ /__/   sh_____ /__/
3. r_____ /__/   thr_____ /__/   gr_____ /__/   fl_____ /__/

Read the short story below, and circle all the words with **ow** that have the /ō/ or /ou/ sound. Then write the words in the correct column below.

Halloween

Tomorrow night the children will go out for Halloween. Although it will be cold, they really hope that it doesn't snow. Tommy will dress up as a clown. Katie will dress up as a princess and wear a beautiful yellow gown and a silver crown on her head. Brian is going to dress up as a ghost and put a large pillowcase over his head. They plan to have their mother drive them around town so they can go trick-or-treating. Katie hopes that she gets bubble gum so she can blow bubbles and teach her brothers how.

4.   /ō/ Sound   5.   /ou/ Sound

   _____   _____
   _____   _____
   _____   _____
   _____   _____
   _____   _____

Vowel Digraph *ow*

Long "O" Sound

Match each clue with a word from the box. Write the words in the puzzle.

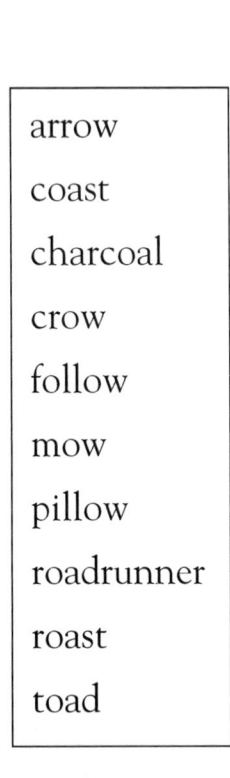

arrow
coast
charcoal
crow
follow
mow
pillow
roadrunner
roast
toad

Across
2. used for resting your head on
3. a froglike amphibian
5. a large, black bird
7. to become very hot; a way of cooking
9. used for barbecuing food
10. to cut down grass

Down
1. the land along an ocean or a sea
4. a pointy stick used for hunting
6. a fast-running desert bird
8. to come or go after

Name _____

The Sounds of "OW"

The letters **ow** can have two sounds. They can have the long o /ō/ sound as in the word *show*, or the /ou/ sound as in the word *plow*.

Match the words with the definitions below. Write the letter of the correct definition on the line.

_____ 1. a, e, i, o, u   **a.** clown

_____ 2. many people together   **b.** shower

_____ 3. small city   **c.** down

_____ 4. tall building   **d.** cow

_____ 5. farm animal   **e.** owl

_____ 6. night bird   **f.** gown

_____ 7. dress   **g.** vowels

_____ 8. not up   **h.** tower

_____ 9. light rain   **i.** town

_____ 10. funny character   **j.** crowd

Now use three **ow** words from above in sentences of your own.

11. _____

12. _____

13. _____

Vowel Digraph *ow*

Sounds of "OU"

The letters **ou** can have many sounds. They can stand for the sounds you hear in these key words: *cloud, touch, soup, would,* and *dough.*

Circle the **ou** word in each sentence. Then write the key word from above on the line that has the same sound as the word you circled.

1. That baby looks too young to be walking. _____

2. I have seen a baby kangaroo in its mother's pouch. _____

3. I wish I could walk on my hands. _____

4. Will you help me with my homework? _____

5. We can go tomorrow, though it might be raining. _____

6. Sometimes I wish we lived in the south. _____

7. May I please get a pet mouse? _____

8. I don't eat meat or poultry. _____

9. Please get into groups so we can start the game. _____

10. It will take me a long time to get through this book. _____

11. I hurt my shoulder playing baseball at recess today. _____

12. My dad always falls asleep on the couch at night. _____

Name _____

"OU" = "OU"

The words below make the /ou/ sound as in the word *loud*.

Match the **ou** words with the definitions below. Write the letter of the correct definition on the line.

_____ 1. shout   a. what you hear

_____ 2. south   b. not quiet

_____ 3. thousand   c. to yell

_____ 4. snout   d. opposite of north

_____ 5. hound   e. the shape of a circle

_____ 6. out   f. where rain falls from

_____ 7. trout   g. a large number

_____ 8. round   h. a type of fish

_____ 9. cloud   i. a hunting dog

_____ 10. loud   j. not in

_____ 11. sound   k. a small pile of dirt

_____ 12. mound   l. the nose and jaws of an animal

13. Read and circle the words that contain the /ou/ sound in this story.

A Dark Cloud

Sam was outside playing on a mound when, suddenly, there was a loud sound that came from a dark cloud! It was thunder! Sam headed south and ran into his house. Max, the family hound, greeted Sam and gave him a nudge with his snout. Instead of playing outdoors, Sam and Max stayed in the house and chased a wound-up toy mouse.

Vowel Digraph *ou*

Name _____

"OW" or "OU"?

Write the letters **ow** or **ou** on the lines to make words. All of the words below make the /ou/ sound.

1. gr_____nd
2. sh_____er
3. f_____nd
4. pl_____
5. h_____se
6. cr_____ded
7. p_____nd
8. am_____nt
9. nightg_____n
10. s_____th

On the lines, write the word that names each picture. Then say the word. Listen for the vowel sounds.

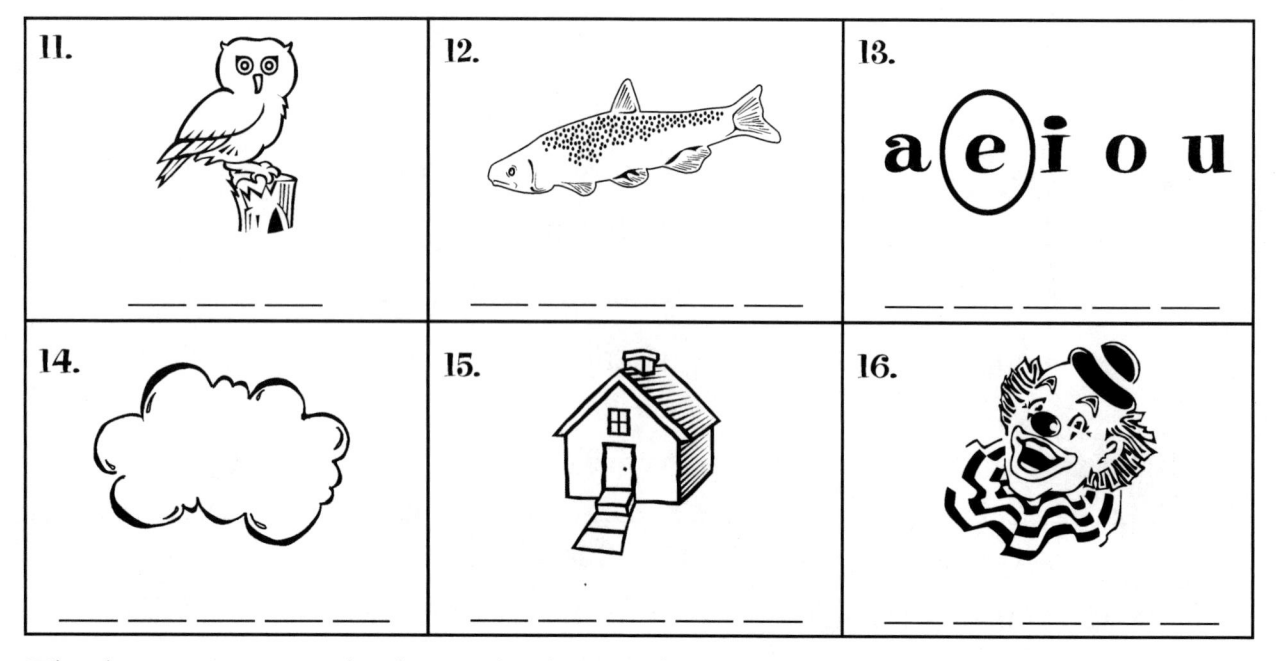

11. _ _ _
12. _ _ _ _ _
13. a (e) i o u _ _ _ _ _
14. _ _ _ _ _
15. _ _ _ _ _
16. _ _ _ _ _

The letters **ou** can also have the long **u** /ū/ sound as in the word *you*.

17. Read and circle the letters that signal the /ū/ sound in each word.

you   youth   soup   group   coupon

156 Daily Skill-Builders Spelling & Phonics 4–5
walch.com © 2004 Walch Publishing

Vowel Digraphs *ow* and *ou*

Name _____

Sound of "AW"

The letters **aw** make the /ô/ sound as in the word *claw*. Read the words. Then circle the letters that signal the /ô/ sound in each word.

1.	hawk	crawl	draw	jaw	flaw
2.	law	saw	fawn	paw	slaw
3.	dawn	yawn	straw	thaw	Shaw
4.	brawl	raw	drawn	spawn	awful

Match the words with the definitions below. Write the letter of the correct definition on the line.

_____ 5. draw   **a.** not cooked

_____ 6. raw   **b.** rules

_____ 7. hawk   **c.** hooked nail on an animal's foot

_____ 8. dawn   **d.** tube to drink from

_____ 9. fawn   **e.** to make pictures

_____ 10. crawl   **f.** the foot of a four-footed animal

_____ 11. paw   **g.** bird

_____ 12. claw   **h.** to move on hands and knees

_____ 13. straw   **i.** early morning

_____ 14. law   **j.** young deer

Vowel Digraph *aw*

Daily Skill-Builders Spelling & Phonics 4–5
walch.com © 2004 Walch Publishing

157

Name _____

"AU" Sentences

The letters **au** make the /ô/ sound as in the first syllable in the word *August*. The **au** spelling does not come at the end of a word. It is found at the beginning and middle of words.

1. Read the words. Then circle the letters that signal the /ô/ sound in each word.

August	vault	Paul	laundry
sauce	haunt	fault	faucet
exhaust	auburn	autograph	automobile

Fill in each line with the word from the box that best completes the sentence.

| faucet | fault | August | autograph |
| laundry | exhausted | haunted | sauce |

2. The plumber will fix the dripping _____.

3. She was born in the month of _____.

4. The fan got a(n) _____ from her favorite musician.

5. Haley is frightened of the _____ house.

6. Matt's dirty clothes need to go into the _____ room.

7. After a full day of sight-seeing, we were _____.

8. It's not my _____ that my homework isn't done.

9. My mom makes the best spaghetti _____.

Name _____

The Sound of "AU" and "AW"

Find the letters that stand for the /ô/ sound in each word. Circle the letters and then write the word on the line next to the correct meaning.

hawk   1. _____ babies do this before they walk

August   2. _____ a car

claw   3. _____ done with a pencil and paper

haunt   4. _____ a bird

exhaust   5. _____ used to grab things

crawl   6. _____ fumes from a car

draw   7. _____ a month

automobile   8. _____ to scare

Now read each sentence. Circle the word with **au** or **aw** that contains the /ô/ sound. Then write the word on the line and circle the letters that represent the /ô/ sound in each word.

9. My dad always wakes up before dawn. _____

10. Will you get me a straw for my drink? _____

11. I have drawn a lot of different comic book characters. _____

12. The exhaust from the car always makes me cough. _____

13. I love her auburn colored hair. _____

14. Don't forget to turn off the faucet. _____

15. My brother Paul plays baseball. _____

16. Mr. Shaw is the best teacher I have ever had. _____

Vowel Digraphs *au* and *aw*

Daily Skill-Builders Spelling & Phonics 4–5
walch.com © 2004 Walch Publishing

159

Name _____

"OI" Versus "OY"

The letters **oi** make the /oi/ sound. The letters **oi** sound like the letters **oy**, but the **oi** spelling is usually used in words or syllables that end in or are followed by consonants.

   Examples: oi   boy

Write the letters **oi** or **oy** on the lines below to complete the words.

   1. t_____   2. b_____l   3. j_____   4. c_____n

   5. r_____al   6. p_____son   7. _____ster   8. p_____nt

Circle the correct spelling of the **oi** and **oy** words in the sentences below.

9. Please flush the (toilet, toylet) and put the seat down.

10. I heard a strange (noise, noyse) come from downstairs in the kitchen.

11. I am trying to (avoid, avoyd) getting sick by drinking a lot of juice.

12. I hope you (enjoi, enjoy) the show.

13. I have never eaten an (oister, oyster).

14. If a big wave comes up on the beach, it will (destroi, destroy) our sand castles.

15. You can do whatever you want; it's your (choice, choyce).

160 Daily Skill-Builders Spelling & Phonics 4–5
walch.com © 2004 Walch Publishing

Vowel Sound /oi/

Name _____

"OI" and "OY"

The letters **oi** and **oy** have the /oi/ sound as in the word *boy*. Fill in each line with the word from the box that best completes the sentence.

foil	choice	soy	destroy	toys
oyster	toiled	noise	enjoy	joined

1. You will have your _____ of great vacation spots.

2. I hope the storm won't _____ our new flower garden.

3. My brother wrapped his leftovers in _____.

4. Today my sister _____ the debate club.

5. The farmers _____ for hours in the hot sun.

6. I hope they _____ their day at the baseball game.

7. We put the baby's favorite _____ in a new storage bin.

8. The small child liked the _____ made by the rattling toy.

9. Do you like _____ sauce on egg rolls?

10. The diver found a pearl inside the _____.

Vowel Sound /oi/

Name _____

Crossing "OY" and "OI"

Match each clue with a word from the box. Write the words in the puzzle.

avoid	destroy	joint	noise	soybean
boil	enjoy	joyful	poison	spoil

Across
1. a plant used for eating
2. happy
4. to make liquid bubbling hot
6. to find pleasure in
8. place where two or more things are joined
9. to stay away from

Down
1. to ruin
3. loud sound
5. dangerous chemical or substance
7. to tear down or demolish

Daily Skill-Builders Spelling & Phonics 4–5
walch.com © 2004 Walch Publishing

Vowel Sound /oi/

Name _____

"IGH" Copycat

The letters **igh** can stand for the long **i** /ī/ sound in words.

Match the words with the definitions below. Write the letter of the correct definition on the line.

____ 1. sigh   **a.** opposite of day

____ 2. light   **b.** way up

____ 3. bright   **c.** breathe aloud

____ 4. high   **d.** opposite of dark

____ 5. might   **e.** correct

____ 6. tight   **f.** ability to see

____ 7. right   **g.** great strength

____ 8. flight   **h.** opposite of loose

____ 9. night   **i.** very shiny

____ 10. sight   **j.** motion in air

Now use the following words in sentences of your own.

| moonlight | nightmare | nightfall | slight |

11. _____

12. _____

13. _____

14. _____

Sound of *igh*

Name _____

Copycat "EIGH"

The letters **eigh** stand for the long a /ā/ sound as in *sleigh*.

Read the words below. Circle only the words that contain the long **a** sound.

1. weight
2. neighbor
3. deceive
4. eight
5. yield
6. freight
7. brief
8. neigh
9. fried

Fill in each line with the word from the box that best completes the sentence.

| eighty | neigh | sleigh | eight | weigh | neighborhoods |

10. My brother is _____ years old and is in the third grade.

11. Although he is short and doesn't _____ much, he is quite nimble.

12. The horse pulls the _____ through the snow-covered countryside.

13. When we pull on the reins, the horse will _____!

14. There are _____ new houses that have been built in my town.

15. There will also be two new _____ in the town.

Daily Skill-Builders Spelling & Phonics 4–5
walch.com © 2004 Walch Publishing

Sound of *eigh*

Name _____

Compound Words

A **compound word** is formed by joining two smaller words together. Read each compound word and write the two words that form it.

1. bookcase _____ _____
2. nosedive _____ _____
3. lifetime _____ _____
4. grandchild _____ _____
5. lighthouse _____ _____
6. snowstorm _____ _____

Now read each sentence. Choose the word that best completes the compound word.

7. Last summer we hiked along the sea_____ in Maine.
   gull   shore   glass

8. I rang the door_____ several times, but no one came to the door.
   knob   mat   bell

9. While on vacation, my sister and I looked for sea_____ on the beach.
   breezes   sides   shells

10. Jason decorated his bed_____ with his favorite posters.
    rock   room   rest

11. My uncle's recipe for home_____ chili is the best I've ever tasted.
    stead   body   made

12. The hikers pitched their tent at a _____ground.
    under   camp   in

Compound Words

Name _____

Grandmother's Visit

Read the words in each column below. Draw lines to match the words that form compound words. Then write the compound words on the lines.

1. grand   line   _____
2. time   vine   _____
3. news   mother   _____
4. grape   mark   _____
5. book   paper   _____

Fill in each line with the word from the box that best completes the sentence.

| airport   birthday   seashore   sunset   afternoon   grandfather   waterfall |

6. I am excited because my grandmother and _____ are coming to visit.

7. I haven't seen them since we spent some time at the _____ together last summer.

8. My dad and I will pick them up at the _____ on Friday evening.

9. While they are visiting, my grandmother will celebrate her seventieth _____.

10. We have planned a special _____ of sightseeing.

11. Then we will go to dinner at a restaurant that overlooks a river and a beautiful _____.

12. Hopefully we'll also get to see a pretty _____.

Name _____

Contraction Time

A **contraction** is a short way to write two words. It is written by putting two words together and leaving out one or more letters. In the place of the letter or letters that are taken out, we put an **apostrophe** (').

Examples: is + not = isn't   we + are = we're   I + will = I'll

Draw lines to match the words on the left with their contractions on the right.

1. it is   a. we'll
2. they are   b. aren't
3. are not   c. it's
4. we will   d. she'll
5. he is   e. they're
6. she will   f. he's

Fill in each line with the contraction from above that best completes the sentence.

7. That boy is much shorter than the other boys, but _____ older than they are.

8. Because you have not done your homework, you _____ allowed to watch television tonight.

9. She always finishes her tests first. _____ be done before _____ finish.

10. _____ not my fault that you do not listen to me.

Contractions

Daily Skill-Builders Spelling & Phonics 4–5
walch.com © 2004 Walch Publishing

167

Name _____

Contractions Again

Read the sentences and circle the words that can be made into contractions. Then write the contractions on the lines.

1. I am not going to the movies tonight. _____

2. You did not call me when you wanted to come home. _____

3. You have been here before, right? _____

4. We went to the mall, but it was not open. _____

5. I should have rented a different game. _____

6. I would like to go pick out a new game to rent. _____

7. She is wearing my favorite sweater today. _____

8. I have always loved that sweater. _____

9. It is blue with yellow flowers all over it. _____

10. You were not at school on time today. _____

11. I just could not get out of bed this morning. _____

12. I have already marked you as absent. _____

Name _____

Contraction Action

Read the contractions below. Write the two words that make up each contraction on the line beside it.

1. they're _____   2. wouldn't _____

3. doesn't _____   4. hasn't _____

5. that's _____   6. you've _____

7. should've _____   8. he'll _____

9. they'll _____   10. weren't _____

Use six of the contractions from above in sentences of your own.

11. _____

12. _____

13. _____

14. _____

15. _____

16. _____

Name _____

More Contractions

Won't is a special contraction. It stands for "will not."

Choose the words from the box below that best complete each sentence. Change the words to contractions before writing them on the lines. Make sure that each sentence makes sense with the contraction.

could not	he will	will not	does not
she is	you are	have not	did not

1. I was sick this morning, so I _____ make it to school.

2. I _____ be going to school tomorrow either.

3. Mrs. Brady knows I am sick, so _____ sending my work home with my neighbor, Paco.

4. _____ bring my work to me when he gets home from school today.

5. I _____ been this sick for a long time.

6. My mom _____ remember the last time I was this sick.

7. My mom said, "_____ going to stay in bed until you feel better."

8. I listened to her. I _____ get out of bed all day.

Contraction Crossword

Read the contractions at the bottom of the page. Write the two words each stands for in the crossword. Do not leave spaces between the words in the crossword puzzle.

Across
3. you've
5. won't
6. I'm
8. aren't
9. wouldn't

Down
1. they'll
2. haven't
3. you're
4. he's
7. you'll

Name _____

That's Mine!

To make a word show ownership, add an apostrophe (') and an **s**. To make a plural word that ends in **s** show ownership, just add the apostrophe.

> the dog   the dog's tail
> Use **'s** when the noun does not end in **s**.
>
> the cats   the cats' tails
> Use the ' (apostrophe) when the noun ends in **s**.

Rewrite each noun to show ownership.

1. Anna _____
2. class _____
3. father _____
4. author _____
5. kittens _____
6. Jeff _____
7. Kim _____
8. horse _____
9. mechanic _____
10. principal _____
11. students _____
12. player _____

Now use five of the possessive nouns above in sentences of your own.

13. _____
14. _____
15. _____
16. _____
17. _____

Singular and Plural Possessives

Name _____

That's Mine, Too!

Rewrite each phrase to show ownership.

1. the hat of the boy _____

2. the desk of the teacher _____

3. the house of my mother _____

4. the books of the girls _____

5. the food for the dog _____

6. the coat Tim has _____

7. the clock at school _____

8. the hair on Sarah _____

9. the fur of the cats _____

10. the voice of the people _____

11. the clothing of the children _____

12. the lessons of the teachers _____

Singular and Plural Possessives

Name _____

Antonyms

An **antonym** is a word that means the opposite of another word.

    Example: small   large

Read the words below. Circle the word that is an antonym of the first word.

1.	early	timely	late	start	finish
2.	light	bare	pale	rough	dark
3.	raw	warm	cooked	wrong	young
4.	fresh	start	thin	stale	firm
5.	friend	wife	relative	love	enemy
6.	nervous	friendly	shy	calm	dull
7.	offer	refuse	reduce	pass	vanish
8.	similar	difficult	common	different	united
9.	failure	sturdy	success	mistake	poor
10.	smile	grin	cry	laugh	frown

Read the words below. Then read the sentences. Complete each sentence by writing the word from the box that is an **antonym** of the underlined word.

guilty	inside	incorrect	stop	forget

11. I'm not sure what time I will <u>start</u> painting, but I know I must _____ by lunchtime.

12. Although the temperature <u>outside</u> was below zero, it was toasty and warm _____.

13. Did Shana <u>remember</u> her homework today or did she _____ it again?

14. Fortunately, the first three math problems were <u>correct</u>, but the last one was _____.

15. The lawyer reminded the jury that a person is <u>innocent</u> until proven _____.

Name _____

Synonyms

A **synonym** is a word that has the same, or nearly the same, meaning as another word.

Example: small   little

Read the words below. Circle the word that means the same or almost the same as the first word.

1. **answer**	page	call	open	reply
2. **locate**	send	find	repeat	final
3. **suggest**	echo	rerun	prepare	propose
4. **repair**	break	mumble	mend	replace
5. **entertain**	dance	amuse	produce	thrill
6. **speed**	haste	miles	crawl	select
7. **choose**	offer	whisper	deny	select
8. **funny**	sad	depressed	comical	friendly
9. **children**	people	youngsters	females	adults
10. **bravery**	soldiers	cowardice	symbol	courage

Read the words below. Then read the sentences and choose a word from the box that is a synonym for the underlined word in the sentence. Write the word on the line.

hurry   exhausted   distant   grateful

11. Some of my friends live in a <u>remote</u> part of the state. _____

12. Each day they have to <u>rush</u> to catch the bus to school. _____

13. By the end of the day, they are often very <u>tired</u>. _____

14. I am certainly <u>thankful</u> that I live so close to school! _____

Synonyms

Daily Skill-Builders Spelling & Phonics 4–5

Name _____

They Sound the Same!

Homophones are words that sound the same but are spelled differently and have different meanings.

   Example: to   too   two

Read the following sentences. Choose the correct word to complete the sentence and write it on the line.

1. My favorite day of the _____ is Friday because I

weak, week

   _____ the weekend is almost _____.
   know, no   hear, here

2. During the weekend I can _____ my friends outside of school,
   sea, see

   and I don't have to worry about any school projects being _____.
   do, due

3. On Saturday mornings I usually wake up _____ before
   right, write

   _____ so I can watch my favorite cartoon.
   ate, eight

4. Sometimes I ride my bike down the _____ to
   road, rode

   _____ my friends at the park.
   meat, meet

5. On some days we spend all afternoon there, but it never

   _____ like that much time has _____.
   seams, seems   passed, past

6. It just isn't _____ that we have to be home by dinner.
   fair, fare

7. _____ stay at the park all day if we had our choice.
   We'd, Weed

8. When we go back to school on Monday, people will _____
   hear, here

   about how we _____ our bikes to the park.
   road, rode

176 *Daily Skill-Builders* Spelling & Phonics 4–5
walch.com © 2004 Walch Publishing

Homophones

Name _____

They Look the Same!

Homographs are words that have the same spelling but different meanings. Sometimes the words are also pronounced differently.

Examples: Please tie that ribbon into a nice **bow**.
In square dancing, the boys **bow** and the girls curtsy.

On the line, write the word from the box that matches the two definitions.

| date | bark | wind | second | ring | tear |
| fan | yard | close | story | lead | rest |

1. comes from the eye; a rip _____
2. after first; a very short time _____
3. floor of a building; a tale _____
4. to relax; what is left _____
5. sweet fruit; day, month, and year _____
6. someone very interested in something; device used to move air _____
7. moving air; to turn _____
8. sound a dog makes; what covers a tree _____
9. sound a phone makes; something that goes on a finger _____
10. near; to shut _____
11. three feet; ground around a house _____
12. to guide; a metal _____

Multiple Meanings

Some words have more than one meaning.

Example: Jim put only one **coat** of paint on the fence.
It's cold outside, so put on a **coat**.

Read each sentence below and use the context of the sentence to figure out the meaning of the word in bold print. Then write the letter of the meaning on the line next to the sentence.

_____ 1. The **principal** of our school has many new ideas about education.
a. a person who heads a school **b.** main; most important

_____ 2. Trying to carry out those ideas might be **hard** because of budget cuts.
a. not soft **b.** difficult

_____ 3. She will **address** those concerns with the school committee.
a. to mark directions for delivery **b.** speak to

_____ 4. To many people, it is **clear** that change is necessary.
a. without clouds or fog **b.** easy to understand

_____ 5. Many of the new ideas are based on what is being done in another **country**.
a. land outside the city **b.** nation

_____ 6. We would have to **spread** the new policies over several years.
a. widen **b.** blanket

_____ 7. It would allow the parents to have a **hand** in planning school events.
a. round of applause **b.** part in doing something

_____ 8. I personally think it is the **right** thing to do.
a. correct **b.** opposite of left

Answer Key

Page 1: Consonant Countdown
1. b, c, d, f, g, h, j, k, l, m, n, p, q, r, s, t, v, w, x, y, z
2. n
3. k
4. z
5. f
6. t
7. c
8. l
9. b
10. d

Page 2: A Box Filled with Consonants
1. dentist, flag, green, baby, cabin
2. joke, mom, ladder (madder), king, number (lumber)
3. rust, video, snake, witch, teeth
4. zoo, yellow, happy, pizza, queen
5. quack, quiet, quite, quick, quiz
6. consonants

Page 3: Missing Consonants
1. bite
2. drip
3. cry
4. help
5. rainbow
6. popcorn, movies
7. trail
8. wax
9. yellow
10. zero

Page 4: Stuck in the Middle
1. toaster, basket
2. apple, baseball
3. haircut, world
4. zigzag, uphill
5. pajamas, firefly
6. thankful, forgot
7. music, preview
8. wristwatch, kennel
9. valley, windmill
10. tuxedo, window

Page 5: In the End
1. pretend; stiff; big, bib, or bid; picnic; cobweb
2. hop; task; album; cabin; ball, balk, or balm
3. buzz, tux, regret, dress, doctor
4. f
5. l
6. r

7–9. Words will vary.

Page 6: Hard and Soft "C"
1. soft
2. soft
3. hard
4. soft
5. soft
6. hard
7. hard
8. soft
9. soft
10. hard

Page 7: Hard and Soft "G"
Soft G: page, magic, giant, gentle, huge, digest, legend

Hard G: garlic, goose, dragon, goat, going

Page 8: Sounding Hard and Soft
1. g
2. s
3. k
4. j
5. j
6. s
7. s
8. g
9. s
10. k
11. j
12. g
13. celery
14. angel
15. orange
16. cereal
17. recess
18. gentle

Page 9: Picturing Hard and Soft Sounds
1. ace /s/
2. crab /k/
3. tiger /g/
4. angel /j/
5. race /s/
6. pig /g/
7. gem /j/
8. cow /k/
9. dragon /g/
10. camera /k/
11. pencil /s/
12. goat /g/

Page 10: Hard or Soft?
1. k
2. g, k
3. s
4. j
5. k
6. g
7. s
8. g
9. k
10. j
11. s
12. j, k
13. s
14. g
15. k
16. g
17. s
18. j
19. k
20. g

Page 11: Puzzling "C" and "G"

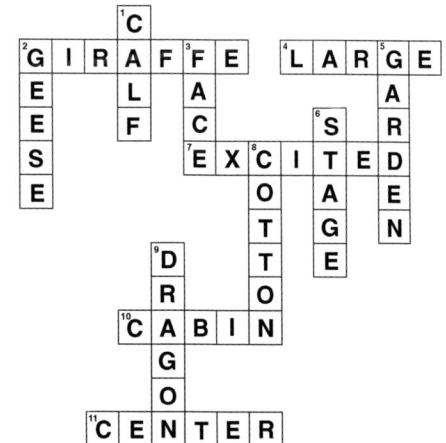

Across: 2. j 4. j 7. s 10. k 11. s
Down: 1. k 2. g 3. s 5. g 6. j 8. k 9. g

Page 12: Two Consonants—One Sound
1. sh, ch, th, wh, ck
2. sh, ch, th, wh, ck
3. sh, ch, th, wh, ck
4. sh, ch, th, wh, ck
5. sh, ch, th, wh, ck

6–10. The digraphs are sh, ch, th, wh, and ck. Words will vary.

Page 13: Quick Digraph Review
Words will vary.
Sample words:
1. kw; queen
2. sh; ship
3. ch; check
4. hw; white
5. th; think
6. ck; stick
7. shot, chick, whip, math
8. shop, shut, that, such
9. stack, then, shed, wick
10. white, thin, there, stack
11. this, than, quiz, clock
12. those, these, church, watch

Page 14: Digraph Search

(word search puzzle)

Page 15: "PH" or "F"?
1. photo
2. correct
3. traffic
4. dolphin
5. fog
6. correct
7. graph
8. alphabet
9. gopher
10. golf
11. orphan
12. correct

Page 16: One Sound—Two Spellings
1. itch
2. sketch
3. teacher
4. punch
5. kitchen
6. switch
7. reach
8. correct
9. pitch
10. correct

Page 17: "PH" and "TCH"
1. dolphin
2. phone
3. trophy
4. elephant
5. catch
6. ketchup
7. scratch
8. witch
9. stretch
10. kitchen
11. ditch
12. switch

Page 18: Searching for Digraphs

(word search puzzle)

Page 19: Two Sounds of "CH"
1. Ch should be circled in all words.
2. Ch should be circled in all words.
3. b
4. c
5. d
6. e
7. a
8. g
9. h
10. f

11–12. Sentences will vary.

Page 20: A "CK" Picnic
1. Arctic, Atlantic, Pacific
2. d
3. c
4. b
5. a
6. comic, septic, rustic, graphic

Page 21: "CK" in the Middle
1. ja*ck*et; c
2. po*ck*et; f
3. lo*ck*et; d
4. cri*ck*et; b
5. pa*ck*et; h
6. ti*ck*et; e
7. ro*ck*et; a
8. ra*ck*et; g

Short Vowel Review

Short vowel sounds are heard when a vowel appears in consonant-vowel-consonant (**CVC**) or vowel-consonant (**VC**) patterns. There can be more than one consonant before or after the vowel.

Examples: căt   bĕd   ĭnch   ŏn   stŭck

Complete the words below by adding the correct vowel on each line.

1. gl___ss   sh___lf   wh___n   bl___st

2. p___nd   cr___st   y___ll   fr___g

3. c___nt___st   c___bw___b   k___tch___n   p___mpk___n

4. m___ff___n   h___pp___n   b___nk b___d   n___pk___n

Write the one-syllable and two-syllable words from above on the lines below.

5. **One-Syllable Words**   6. **Two-Syllable Words**

_____   _____
_____   _____
_____   _____
_____   _____
_____   _____
_____   _____
_____   _____
_____   _____

Name _____

Long Vowel Review

There are two types of syllables in which long vowel sounds are heard.
Remember: Long vowel sounds say their names.

Open syllables are syllables that end in a vowel. Examples are **he, hi, go, flu,** and the first syllable heard in the word *April*. When the letter **y** comes at the end of a one-syllable word, it makes the long **i** sound. When the letter **y** comes at the end of a word with two or more syllables, it usually makes the long **e** sound.

Examples: cry /ī/   baby /ē/

Complete the words below by adding the correct vowel on each line.

1. wh___   n___   z___r___   dizz___
2. ponch___   fift___   ___pen   b___gin
3. t___lip   r___lax   m___son   m___self

Silent-e syllables follow a vowel-consonant-e (**VCe**) pattern. The vowel before the consonant is usually long, and the final **e** is silent.

Examples: cake   Pete   bike   home   mule   rule

Complete the words below by adding the correct vowel.

4. h___pe   scr___pe   h___ge   h___de
5. exc___se   expl___de   clockw___se   h___meroom
6. infl___te   uns___fe   rept___le   cupc___ke
7. tadp___le   cost___me   tromb___ne   ins___de

Page 22: What's at the End?
1. dunk, bring, wing
2. thank, chunk
3. string, sang
4. lung, link, long
5. ng or nk, nk, nk, nk
6. ng, ng, nk, nk, ng
7. ng, nk or ng, nk, nk, ng

8–10. Sentences will vary.

Page 23: Picture This!
1. skunk
2. king
3. sink
4. drink
5. wing
6. bank
7. ring
8. bank
9. bunk
10. hang, sink
11. think, pink
12. sang

Page 24: "NG" or "NK"?
1. ping-pong
2. sank
3. bunk
4. strong
5. sang
6. song
7. stung
8. hang
9. thank
10. sink
11. Honk
12. ring

Page 25: A Final Letter
1. dress, doll, mess, shell
2. off, chess, sell, stuff
3. Will, stuff, sill
4. still, mess
5. huff, hill
6. pass, shells
7. doll
8. Miss, will, chess
9. ball, tall, mall, fall, wall, call

Page 26: Add a Letter
Words circled:
1. bell, will
2. Miss, Bess
3. will, mall
4. moss, tall
5. Bill, will, sell, chess, mall
6. off, hill, fall
7. toss, ball, doll
8. Jill's, dress, mess

9–12. Sentences will vary.

Page 27: Sounds in a Name
1. T o m
2. T i m
3. B o b
4. B i ll
5. Ch e t
6. J o sh
7. R o b
8. B e th
9. J e ff
10. J i ll
11. Ch a d
12. T e d
13. D e b
14. J a ck
15. K i m
16. L i z
17. N i ck
18. R i ch
19. R o ss
20. B e v
21. B e n
22. K e n
23. J e d
24. P a t
25. R o z
26. D o n
27. P e g
28. R i ck
29. S e th
30. M e g
31. J u d
32. B e ss
33. K r i s
34. C l i ff

Page 28: Blend Together
1. blue, brick, cry
2. sting, skin, true
3. plate, price, frog
4. drink, flock, swim
5. green, spine, scar
6. snake, glad, clock

Page 29: Beginning Blends
1. sting, sling, bring, swing, cling
2. stand, brand, bland, gland, grand
3. black, stack, snack, track, slack
4. brick, stick, flick, trick, slick
5. stock, flock, clock, block, crock
6. pl, cr, bl, br, gl
7. tr, sn, sl, tw, cr
8. cl, sw, sp, fl, sc

9–10. Sentences will vary.

Page 30: Blends, Blends, and More Blends
1. scr, scr, shr
2. str, str, shr
3. spl, spl, nch
4. scr, scr, nch
5. str, nch, nch
6. scr, nch, str
7. lunch
8. stream
9. scribble
10. street

Page 31: Blends at the End
1. blond
2. fast
3. shelf
4. milk
5. desk
6. belt
7. held
8. jump
9. bl, nd; cr, ft; br, sk; cl, mp; tr, st
10. cr, st; fr, st; cl, sp; st, mp; sp, nd

184 Daily Skill-Builders Spelling & Phonics 4–5

Page 32: Begin with Blends

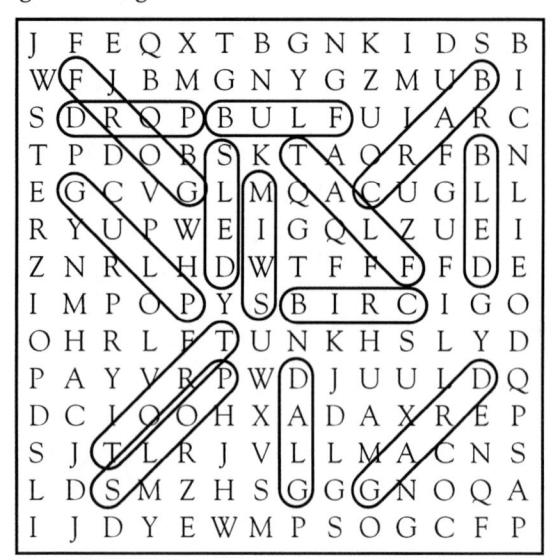

```
J F E Q X T B G N K I D S B
W F I B M G N Y G Z M U B I
S D R O P B U L F U J A R C
T P D O B S K T A Q R F B N
E G C V G L M Q A C U G L L
R Y U P W E I G O L Z U E I
Z N R L H D W T F F F D H E
I M P O P Y S B I R C I G O
O H R L F T U N K H S L Y D
P A Y V R P W D J U U L D Q
D C L O O H X A D A X R E P
S J T L R J V L L M A C N S
L D S M Z H S G G G N O Q A
I J D Y E W M P S O G C F P
```

Page 33: Now, End with Blends

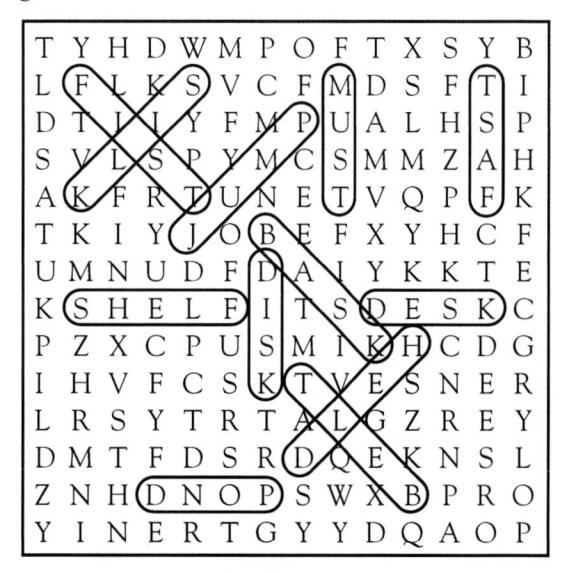

```
T Y H D W M P O F T X S Y B
L F L K S V C F M D S F T I
D T I I Y F M P U A L H S P
S V L S P Y M C S M M Z A H
A K F R T U N E T V Q P F K
T K I Y J O B E F X Y H C F
U M N U D F A I Y K K T E
K S H E L F I T S D E S K C
P Z X C P U S M I K H C D G
I H V F C S K T V E S N E R
L R S Y T R T A L G Z R E Y
D M T F D S R D Q E K N S L
Z N H D N O P S W X B P R O
Y I N E R T G Y Y D Q A O P
```

Page 34: The "K" Is Silent
1. Kn should be circled in each word, and k should be crossed out in each word.
2. knows
3. knuckle, knocked
4. knees
5. knapsack
6. knob

Page 35: That Quiet "W"!
1. Wr should be circled in each word, and w should be crossed out in each word.
2. write
3. wrong
4. written
5. wrinkle
6. wreck
7. wrist
8. wrap
9. wrote
10. wreath

Page 36: Silent "B"
1. yes
2. no
3. yes
4. yes
5. yes
6. no
7. no
8. yes
9. no
10–11. Sentences will vary.

Page 37: A Simple Pattern
1. băg, kĭt, pĕt, ĭll, săck
2. bĕd, cŭt, fŏx, gŏt, chĭp
3. yĕll, pŏp, bŭg, ŏff, jŭmp
4. mŭd, ĭn, wĕd, dĕn, shŏck
5. short
6. ˘

Page 38: Picturing Short Vowels
1. e
2. u
3. a
4. i
5. o
6. e
7. a
8. o
9. u

Page 39: They're All Short
1. gŭm
2. bĕd
3. snăck
4. spŏt
5. bĕll
6. chĭp
7. măth
8. shŭt
9. drŏp
10. quĭck

Page 40: A Missing Vowel
1. bask
2. disk
3. held
4. belt
5. blond
6. crust
7. golf
8. elf
9. bulk
10. weld
11. disk
12. mask
13. blast
14. jump
15. shelf
16. bump
17. a, e, i, o, u

Page 41: Short "A," Short "I"
1. Jim, will
2. will, swim
3. cat, fast
4. ship
5. Dad, fix
6. grass, trim
7. Brad, will
8. cap
9. cat, fast, Dad, grass, Brad, cap
10. Jim, will, swim, ship, fix, trim

Page 42: Short "O," Short "U"
1. Bob, not, job
2. not, stub, tub

3. pup, lost, fog
4. spot, rug
5. lock, dusk
6. Tom, bugs
7. must, not, fox
8. frog, jump
9. Bob, not, job, lost, fog, spot, lock, Tom, fox, frog
10. stub, tub, pup, rug, dusk, bugs, must, jump

Page 43: Fill in the Vowels
1. fast, fist
2. sell, sill
3. mass, mess, miss, moss, muss
4. bag, beg, big, bog, bug
5. dig, dog, dug
6. cat, cot, cut
7. mad, mid, mud
8. cap, cop, cup
9. fat, fit
10. sack, sick, sock, suck
11. red, rid, rod
12. stack, stick, stock, stuck

Page 44: Short Vowel Review
1. bask, weld, staff, dress, nest, clasp, stack, best, help, that, snap, scrap, swam
2. fist, boss, plug, twig, frost, dust, shrimp, crisp, which, bulk, crop, spill, milk

Page 45: Rhyme Time
1. web, Deb; red, fed; beg, leg; men, ten
2. mob, sob; fog, log; hot, got; box, fox
3. bat, cat; cap, gap; bag, rag; mad, sad
4. hid, lid; bit, fit; hip, dip; dim, him
5. gum, hum; bug, dug; bud, mud; but, cut
6. belt, felt; blast, fast; blond, pond; bust, crust
7. CVC

Page 46: "A" with "M" and "N"
1. All words except for *fram, stam, gramper* should be circled.
2. All words except *pran, yan, spran, crand, drant* should be circled.
3. stand, cramp, strand, scram, clamp, branch
4. chant, clam or clan, hamper, slant, band, slam
5. fan
6. clam
7. man
8. stamp

Page 47: "AM" or "AN"?
1. ham, pan
2. Jan, tan
3. fan
4. Pam, ran

5. van
6. Sam, swam, than, Dan
7. plan, jam
8. Tam, camp
9. ham, Pam, Sam, swam, jam, Tam, camp
10. pan, Jan, tan, fan, ran, van, than, Dan, plan

Page 48: Breaking Rules
1. sōld, wīld, lŏst, mōst, hīnd, mōlt
2. cŏst, find, ōld, kīnd, behīnd, mīnd
3. most
4. wild
5. find
6. molts
7. mind
8. kinds

Page 49: Breaking Rules Again
1. old, kind
2. colt
3. sold
4. mild
5. told
6. most
7. find
8. hold, child
9. cōld
10. pōst
11. wīld
12. hōst
13. mīld
14. vōlt
15. hīnd
16. bōld

Page 50: The Schwa
1. o
2. o
3. e (second)
4. i
5. u
6. o
7. e
8. o
9. a
10. e
11. o
12. o (second)

Page 51: Searching for Schwa

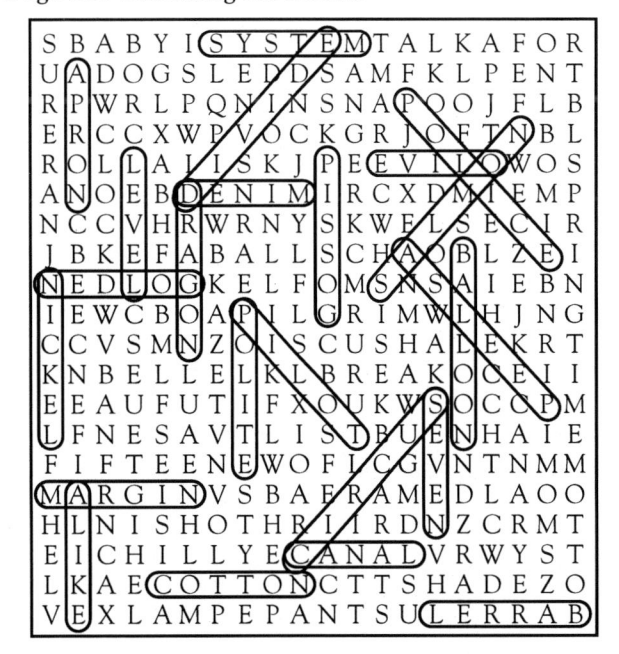

Page 52: Open and Long
1. nō; O
2. bĕd; NO
3. flū; O
4. mē; O
5. shē; O
6. dŏg; NO
7. kĭd; NO
8. sŭn; NO
9. bē; O
10. /ī/
11. /ē/
12. /ī/
13. /ō/
14. /ī/
15. /ī/
16–18. Sentences will vary.

Page 53: More Open Syllables
1. flu
2. She
3. I, fly
4. try
5. me
6. cry
7. my
8. go
9. ē, ī, ī, ō, ū
10. ē, ō, ī, ō, ī

Page 54: When "Y" Sounds Like Long "E"
1. candy
2. puppy
3. baby
4. lady
5. bunny
6. kitty
7. tidy
8. ruby
9. sandy
10. plenty
11. sil lē
12. hob bē
13. fun nē
14. hol lē
15. hap pē
16. pen nē

Page 55: Ends with "Y"
1. ruby
2. Molly
3. lady
4. sunny
5. buddy
6. messy
7. lazy
8. funny
9. sandy
10. fifty

Page 56: Names Ending in "Y"
1. Bil lē
2. Sam mē
3. Man dē
4. Tom mē
5. Mis sē
6. Co dē
7. To bē
8. Mol lē
9. To nē
10. Min dē
11. Betsy
12. Krissy
13. Holly
14. Robby
15. Sally
16. Bobby
17. Jenny
18. Patty
19. Peggy
20. Judy

Page 57: The Silent "E"
2. cŭb, cūbe
3. tŭb, tūbe
4. dĭm, dīme
5. hĭd, hīde
6. bĭt, bīte
7. căn, cāne
8. cŏp, cōpe
9. hŏp, hōpe
10. rĭd, rīde
11. cŭt, cūte
12. hăt, hāte
13. scrăp, scrāpe
14. strĭp, strīpe
15. slĭd, slīde
16. plăn, plāne
17. slŏp, slōpe
18. spĭn, spīne

Page 58: Shh! Silent "E"
1. plane
2. bone
3. nine
4. mule
5. skate
6. house
7. cone
8. bike
9. flute
10. cake
11. phone
12. fire

Page 59: A Word or Not a Word?
2. plane, plan; scrape, scrap
3. maze, blank; cane, can
4. safe, blank; brave, blank
5. dive, blank; slide, slid
6. spine, spin; bike, blank
7. life, blank; mile, blank
8. bite, bit; dime, dim
9. hope, hop; bone, blank
10. home, blank; phone, blank
11. vote, blank; globe, glob
12. cope, cop; broke, blank
13. tune, blank; cube, cub
14. cute, cut; rule, blank
15. mule, blank; prune, blank
16. tube, tub; flute, blank

Page 60: Breaking Even More Rules
1. ĭ
2. ī
3. ī
4. ĭ
5. ī
6. ī, ĭ
7. ŭ
8. ō
9. ŭ
10. ō

Page 61: When "S" Sounds Like "Z"
1. nōz
2. hōz
3. wīz
4. rīz
5. rōz
6. thēz
7. thōz
8. pōz
9. fūz
10. ūz
11. nose
12. rose
13. pose
14. rise
15. wise
16. use, hose

Daily Skill-Builders Spelling & Phonics 4–5

Page 62: Searching for Silent "E"

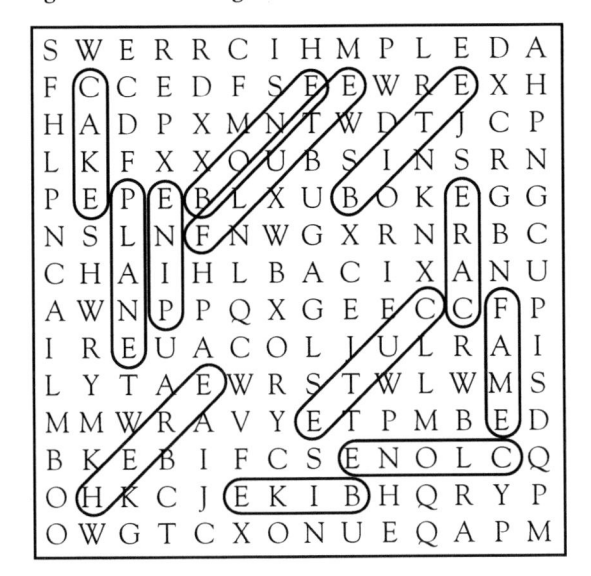

Page 63: More Than One
1. con test
2. com bat
3. him self
4. fin ish
5. pub lic
6. suf fix
7. den tist
8. tab let
9. nap kin
10. pump kin
11. trum pet
12. snap shot
13. wit ness
14. ex press
15. chip munk

Page 64: Adding Closed Syllables
2. tălĕnt
3. sŭmmĭt
4. tŏnsĭl
5. prŏblĕm
6. cŏbwĕb
7. ŭnpăck
8. cănnŏt
9. plăstĭc
10. fŏssĭl
11. pŭmpkĭn
12. cŏntĕst

Page 65: Two-Syllable Words
1. muffin
2. pumpkin
3. trumpet
4. sandwich
5. picnic
6. cobweb
7. dentist
8. cactus
9. magnet
10. basket

Page 66: Complete the Sentences
1. problem
2. unpack
3. Unlock
4. pumpkin
5. pollen
6. picnic
7. hopscotch
8. cotton
9. contest
10. sandwich

Page 67: Making It Real
1. dentist, picnic, object, trumpet
2. pumpkin, cannot, happen, gossip
3. dentist, picnic, object, trumpet, pumpkin, cannot, happen, gossip

4–8. Sentences will vary.

Page 68: Three-Syllable Words
1. făntăstĭc
2. ĭnhăbĭt
3. băskĕtbăll
4. pĕnmănshĭp
5. măgnĕtĭc
6. Wĭscŏnsĭn
7. crăftsmănshĭp
8. Thănksgĭvĭng
9. cŏnsĭstĕnt
10. dĭsĭnfĕct

Page 69: Syllable Division
1. in hale
2. ex hale
3. in vite
4. tad pole
5. trom bone
6. cup cake
7. turn pike
8. bed time
9. dis like
10. cos tume
11. in side
12. base ball
13. spring time
14. milk shake
15. pan cake
16. mis take
17. ex plode
18. base ment

Page 70: Finish Your Sentence
1. tadpole
2. trombone
3. turnpike
4. escape
5. airplane
6. pancake
7. combine
8. fireman
9. homesick
10. baseball
11. costume
12. improve

Page 71: Syllable Combinations
1. rĕptīle
2. cŭpcāke
3. fīremăn
4. trŏmbōne
5. păncāke
6. bāsebăll
7. cŏstūme
8. mĭlkshāke

Pictures and words should be marked correctly.

Page 72: Connect the Syllables
1. mistake, careless, exhale, pancake
2. springtime, unsafe, dislike, homesick
3. mistake, careless, exhale, pancake, springtime, unsafe, dislike, homesick

4–8. Sentences will vary.

Page 73: More Three-Syllable Words
1. rĕcŏgnīze
2. dĕmŏnstrāte
3. ĭncŏmplēte
4. dĭstrĭbūte
5. cŏntĕmplāte
6. demonstrate
7. distribute
8. incomplete
9. recognize
10. contemplate

Page 74: Open and Closed
1. sēcrĕt
2. bēgăn
3. prētĕnd
4. frōzĕn
5. mȳsĕlf
6. rēlăx
7. hōtĕl
8. mōtĕl
9. stūdĕnt
10. hūmĭd
11. spōkĕn
12. rōdĕnt

Page 75: Banjo Music
1. băn + jō
2. mū + sĭc
3. student, music
4. begin
5. frozen
6. mason
7. relax
8. banjo
9. hotel

Page 76: Open or Closed?

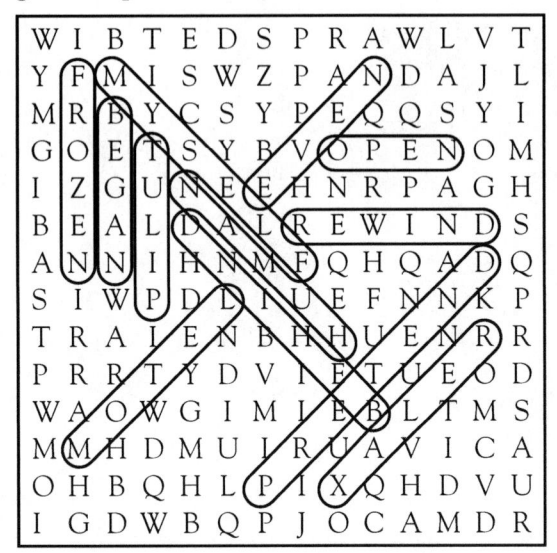

```
W I B T E D S P R A W L V T
Y F M I S W Z P A N D A J L
M R B Y C S Y P E Q Q S Y I
G O E T S Y B V O P E N O M
I Z G U N E E H N R P A G H
B E A L D A L R E W I N D S
A N N I H N M F Q H Q A D Q
S I W P D L I U E F N N K P
T R A L E N B H U E N R E
P R R T Y D V I E T U E O D
W A O W G I M L E B L T M S
M M H D M U I R U A V I C A
O H B Q H L P I X Q H D V U
I G D W B Q P J O C A M D R
```

Page 77: More Open Syllables
2. sī lō
3. zē rō
4. ē mū
5. bā by, /bē/
6. hā lo
7. bō ny, /nē/
8. crā zy, /zē/
9. sō lō
10. rū by, /bē/

Page 78: Open-Syllable Words
1. ho + ly
2. he + ro
3. ve + to
4. ti + ny
5. na + vy
6. ze + ro
7. ha + lo
8. ba + by
9. ti + dy
10. e + mu
11. tu + tu
12. po + ny
13. ha + zy
14. so + lo

15–18. Sentences will vary.

Page 79: Open and Silent "E"
1. dēcīde
2. prōmōte
3. ōzōne
4. rōtāte
5. lōcāte
6. bēsīde
7. pōlīte
8. bēhāve
9. mīgrāte
10. rēmōte
11. remote
12. polite
13. migrate
14. decide
15. behave

Page 80: It Ends with "LE"
2. candle, short
3. little, short
4. title, long
5. puzzle, short
6. cable, long
7. bottle, short
8. middle, short
9. noble, long
10. sample, short

Page 81: Separating "LE"
2. pic kle
3. ma ple
4. un cle
5. sim ple
6. puz zle
7. ca ble
8. mus cle
9. chuck le
10. fid dle
11. lit tle, dim ple
12. ti tle, driz zle, jun gle
13. buck le, set tle
14. can dle, ta ble
15. a ble, whis tle

Page 82: "S" or "Z" Sound?
1. flames, /z/
2. bats, /s/
3. sings, /z/
4. hops, /s/
5. ships, /s/
6. canes, /z/
7. flutes, /s/
8. dads, /z/
9. hugs, /z/
10. hills, /z/
11. bikes, /s/
12. snakes, /s/
13. helps, /s/
14. baths, /s/
15. handcuffs, /s/
16. reptiles, /z/
17. vampires, /z/
18. handshakes, /s/
19. flagpoles, /z/
20. cupcakes, /s/

Page 83: Making It Plural
1. cakes
2. bugs
3. rings
4. beds
5. gloves
6. phones
7. cameras
8. feathers
9. boots

10–11. Sentences will vary.

Page 84: When to Add "ES"
1. taxes, lunches, matches, brushes, messes
2. axes, benches, witches, splashes, misses
3. boxes, munches, crutches, wishes, fusses
4. fixes, inches, stitches, flashes, bosses

5–8. Sentences will vary.

Page 85: Adding "S" or "ES"
1. matches
2. dishes
3. chairs
4. benches
5. brushes
6. boxes
7. keys
8. rings
9. sandwiches
10. witches
11. roses
12. axes

Page 86: "S" or "ES"?
1. es, dishes
2. s, mugs
3. es, riches
4. es, buses
5. s, songs
6. s, falls
7. es, pinches
8. es, guesses
9. s, bikes
10. s, plays
11. es, boxes
12. es, rashes

Page 87: "Y" to "I"
1. cities, parties, countries, agencies, spies, enemies, companies, duties
2. keys, donkeys, holidays, plays, chimneys, Mondays, boys

Page 88: It Ends in "O"
1. Kangaroos
2. tomatoes
3. pianos
4. Eskimos, igloos
5. heroes
6. radios
7. rodeos
8. stereos

Page 89: From "F" to "V"
1. elves
2. loaves
3. wives
4. halves
5. leaves
6. lives
7. shelves
8. scarves
9. loaves
10. scarf
11. leaves
12. shelf
13. lives
14. halves

Page 90: So Irregular
1. children
2. moose
3. women
4. teeth
5. fish
6. mice
7. sheep
8. feet
9. geese
10. deer
11. teeth
12. feet
13. children
14. fish
15. sheep

Page 91: Reviewing Plurals
1. radios
2. parties
3. scarves
4. moose
5. holidays
6. knives
7. mice
8. heroes
9. babies
10. teeth
11. igloos
12. halves
13. stereos
14. donkeys
15. calves
16. feet
17. women
18. kangaroos
19. enemies
20. lives

Page 92: "ING" Action
1. fish, box, rest, sing, sleep
2. jump, add, yell, golf, think
3. bank, bring, pack, sell, miss
4. fishing
5. yelling
6. jumping
7. sleeping
8. missing
9. packing
10. singing

Page 93: Adding "ING" to Silent "E"
1. baking
2. making
3. biking
4. hoping
5. giving
6. diving
7. joke
8. save
9. shine
10. rise
11. move
12. shake
13. saving
14. moving
15. hoping
16. diving
17. shining
18. biking

Page 94: Finishing Sentences
1. golfing
2. dressing
3. jumping
4. resting
5. locking
6. folding
7. hiking
8. baking
9. making
10. living

Page 95: Adding "ING" to CVC Words
1. napping
2. running
3. shopping
4. hopping
5. hope
6. bank
7. sled
8. love
9. ship
10. walk
11. bike
12. chat
13. M, quitting
14. M, baking
15. C
16. C
17. M, writing
18. M, jumping

Page 96: Put It in the Past
Circled words: folded, melted, rested, hunted, pretended, twisted, distracted, disrupted
Underlined words: stamped, wished, crossed
Boxed words: yelled, brushed, called
1. pretended
2. melted
3. hunted
4. disrupted
5. folded

Page 97: What Do You Hear?
1. /d/, /t/
2. /t/, /ed/
3. /t/
4. /d/, /t/
5. /t/
6. /d/
7. /d/, /ed/
8. /t/, /t/, /d/
9. /d/, /t/
10. /t/

Page 98: Silent "E" Past
1. ed, timed
2. ed, liked
3. ed, biked
4. ed, saved
5. ed, hoped
6. ed, skated
7. ed, tired
8. ed, baked
9. ed, scared
10. ed, dared
11. skated
12. tired

13. raked
14. poked
15. ruled

Page 99: CVC and "ED"
1. tapped
2. ripped
3. jogged
4. chopped
5. batted
6. hugged
7. popped
8. dropped

Page 100: Three Sounds of "ED"
1. ed, crunched, /t/
2. ed, thrilled, /d/
3. ed, helped, /t/
4. ed, dusted, /ed/
5. ed, called, /d/
6. ed, tricked, /t/
7. ed, jelled, /d/
8. ed, hiked, /t/

9–12. Sentences will vary.

Page 101: Crossing "ED"

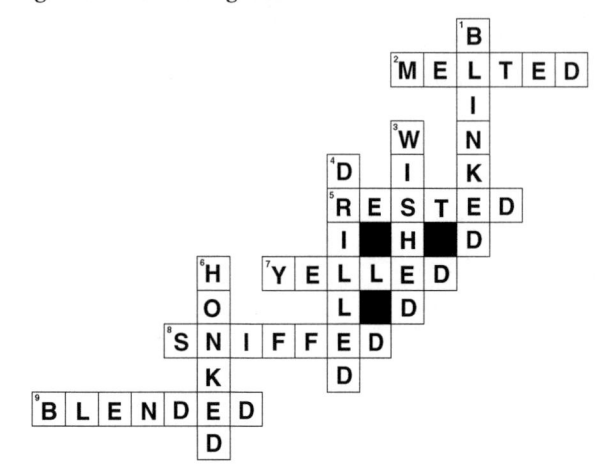

Crossword:
1. BLINKED
2. MELTED
3. WINK
4. DIK
5. RESTED
6. HONK
7. YELLED
8. SNIFFED
9. BLENDED

Page 102: The Meaning of "ER"
1. er, kinder, more
2. er, sicker, more
3. er, worker, person
4. er, thinker, person
5. er, colder, more
6. er, painter, person
7. er, slower, more
8. er, teacher, person
9. er, builder, person
10. er, thicker, more

Page 103: Breaking "ER" Rules
1. er, cuter
2. er, giver
3. er, dancer
4. er, safer
5. er, ruler
6. braver
7. voter
8. baker
9. skater
10. wider

Page 104: Adding "ER" to "Y"
1. scarier
2. hairier
3. tinier
4. tidier
5. happier
6. sillier
7. prettier
8. funnier

9–12. Sentences will vary.

Page 105: "ER" and CVC Words
1. slimmer
2. batter
3. hotter
4. runner
5. bigger
6. chatter
7. fatter
8. jogger
9. sadder
10. flatter
11. wrapper

Page 106: What Does "EST" Mean?
1. faster
2. tallest
3. older
4. quickest
5. coldest
6. longer
7. deeper
8. highest
9. thickest
10. smaller

Page 107: Breaking "EST" Rules
1. est, safest
2. est, bravest
3. est, widest
4. est, closest
5. est, nicest
6. latest
7. cutest
8. whitest
9. purest
10. rudest

Page 108: Searching for More and Most

```
W U T H E H L I S H A P P Y
T Y A N E O W T T R B D J P
O K U X W E S R S E R Z P J
A L L I E X V E D A L F S
B Y A D D J S B G L V T T X
I Z E L E T X H N O E I Z W
P R I Y L G N R O B S P F P
M W T H I C K E R P T A R
Z K W E A Z X B T K P E W E
E R E I Z A L H S D K E A T
S Y L S H I D K D O L A R K
Q C F Q J T M M J G Y Q A A
M V Z J P Z D J M A F V J Z
O P H Y E W X Q M F L W Z E
```

Page 109: Prefix Power
1. unsafe
2. unload
3. unfair
4. unhappy
5. unpack

6–10. Sentences will vary.

Page 110: Before and Again
1. refill
2. preheat
3. reread
4. rewrite
5. prepay
6. replay
7. pregame
8. preschool
9. preheat
10. reread
11. replay
12. preschool

13. refill
14. pregame
15. rewrite
16. prepay

Page 111: Prefixes Again
1. nonfat
2. misspell
3. misunderstood
4. nonfiction
5. misbehave
6. misplaced
7. nonstop
8. nonsense

Page 112: Is That Too Much?
1. overeat
2. impatient
3. overcharged
4. overheat
5. improper
6. oversleep
7. overeat; eat too much
8. impatient; not patient
9. overcharged; charged too much
10. overheat; heat too much

Page 113: Prefixes Across and Down

(crossword with answers: DISAGREE, MISBEHAVE, NONSTOP, REFILL, IMPATIENT, UNLOCK; downs include PRE, PREVIEW, MAD, OVERSLEEP, PUFFY, etc.)

Page 114: What Does "LESS" Mean?
1. mindless
2. restless
3. helpless
4. hopeless
5. boneless
6. spineless
7. lifeless
8. homeless
9. nameless
10. wireless
11. boneless
12. homeless, restless
13. restless
14. helpless
15. useless

Page 115: What Does "FUL" Mean?
1. helpful, full of help
2. hopeful, full of hope
3. thankful, full of thanks
4. careful, full of care
5. respectful, full of respect
6. painful, full of pain
7. painful
8. careful
9. helpful
10. respectful
11. thankful
12. hopeful

Page 116: Finding "LESS" and "FUL"

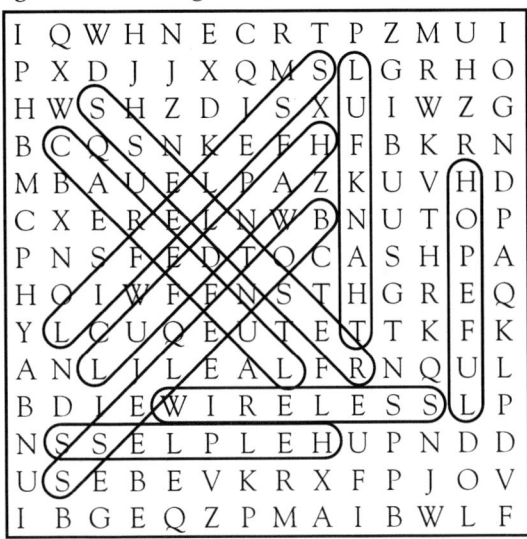

(word search puzzle)

Page 117: It Ends with "Y"
1. y, lucky
2. ly, lonely
3. y, handy
4. ly, lately
5. y, messy
6. ly, lovely
7. ly, quickly
8. lucky
9. messy
10. lovely
11. quickly

Page 118: Why Suffixes?

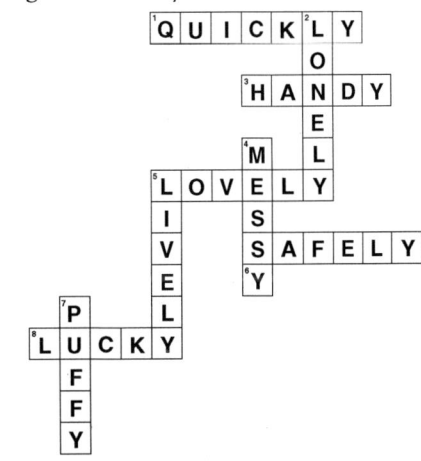

(crossword with answers: QUICKLY, HANDY, LOVELY, SAFELY, LUCKY; downs include LONELY, MESSY, LIVELY, PUFFY)

Page 119: "TION"
1. prevention—act of preventing
2. relaxation—act of resting
3. location—a position or site
4. construction—act of building
5. dictation—act of speaking
6. production—something produced
7. infection—a state of disease
8. direction—guidance or instruction

9–10. Sentences will vary.

Page 120: Making "TION" Words
2. invitation
3. vacation
4. addition
5. solution
6. education
7. prediction
8. invention

Page 121: Another "ION" Suffix
1. zhŭn
2. zhŭn
3. zhŭn
4. zhŭn
5. zhŭn
6. zhŭn
7. shŭn
8. shŭn
9. zhŭn
10. zhŭn
11. shŭn
12. shŭn
13. mansion
14. television
15. explosion
16. invasion
17. division
18. decision

Page 122: "TION" or "SION"?

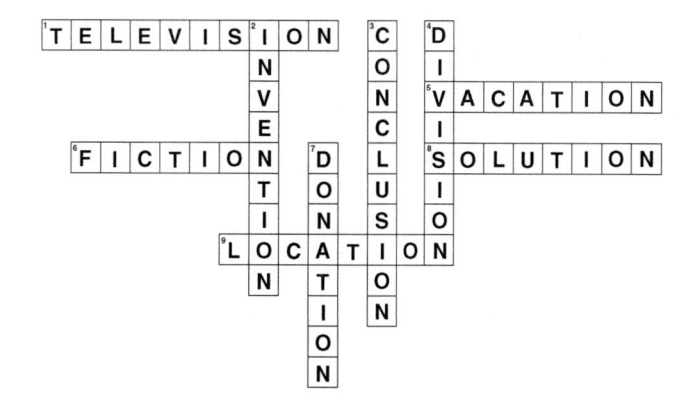

1 across: TELEVISION
6 across: VACATION
6 down/across: FICTION
8 across: SOLUTION
9 across: LOCATION
(with intersecting words: INVENTION, CONCLUSION, DIVISION, ILLUSION, OPTION, NATION, CAUTION)

Page 123: "ANCE" or "ENCE"?
1. attendance; act of attending
2. audience; act of hearing
3. clearance; act of clearing
4. silence; act of being silent
5. intelligence; state of being intelligent
6. acceptance; act of being accepted

Page 124: "ANCE" and "ENCE" Sentences
1. science
2. performance
3. attendance
4. audience
5. allowance
6. violence
7. assistance
8. silence
9. confidence
10. appearance

Page 125: Wrap It Up!
Possible answers:
1. es, boxes
2. y, messy
3. ful, thankful
4. ing, swinging
5. less, wireless
6. er, stronger
7. ed, hugged
8. ly, lonely
9. ty, sixty
10. est, quickest

Sentences will vary.

Page 126: That Controlling "R"!
New words will vary; the following words should be circled:
1. stars
2. short
3. circus
4. burp
5. mother
6. artist
7. corn
8. nurse
9. pepper
10. thirty

Page 127: Picturing "AR"
1. dart
2. star
3. harp
4. car
5. shark
6. barn
7. yarn
8. cart
9. scarf

10–12. Sentences will vary.

Page 128: Picturing "OR"
1. corn
2. horse
3. fork
4. storm
5. forty
6. cord
7. horn
8. thorn
9. torch

10–12. Sentences will vary.

Page 129: "AR" and "OR" Rulebreakers
1. ar, /er/
2. or, /er/
3. or, /er/
4. ar, /er/
5. or, /er/
6. or, /er/
7. ar, /er/
8. ar, /er/
9. or, /er/
10. or, /er/
11. ar, /er/
12. ar, /er/
13. or, /er/
14. ar, /er/
15. ar, /er/
16. or, /er/

17–20. Sentences will vary.

Page 130: "ER" Sound
1. her, monster, banker, sticker, sister, hamster
2. stir, fir, sir, dirt, flirt, birth
3. blur, fur, spur, curl, hurt, curb

4–9. Sentences will vary.

Page 131: "ER," "IR," or "UR"?
1. brother, member, girl
2. silver, sunburn, survive
3. mother, dirty, return
4. disturb, verb, swirl
5. birth, shirt, burst
6. occur, chirp, lurk
7. bakery, thunder, burp
8. termite, summer, number
9. her, church, squirm
10. hamster, fern, Germany

Page 132: You're In Control!

The following letters should be circled:

1. er, ar, or, or
2. or, er, er, er
3. or, or, ar, ar
4. ur, er, ir, ur
5. er, er, ur, ar
6. energy, morning
7. first
8. person
9. forty
10. boring, cartoons

Page 133: R-Controlled Clues

1. circle
2. turkey
3. barks
4. cartoon
5. garden
6. slippers
7. birthday
8. hornet
9. fork
10. morning
11. picture
12. teacher

Page 134: Controlling Crossword

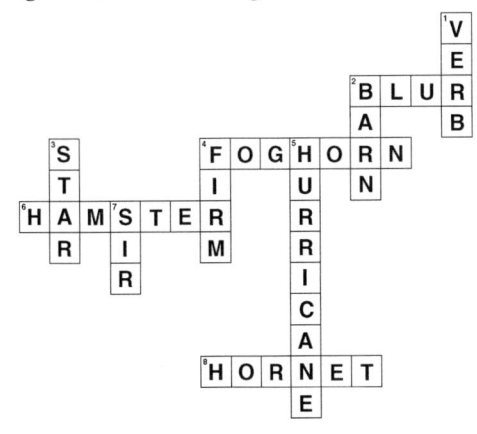

[Crossword grid with answers: VERB, BLURB, BAB, STIRRUP, FOGHORN, HAMSTER, HURRICANE, HORNET]

Page 135: "AY" Sentences

1. way
2. jay
3. clay
4. delay
5. ray
6. stray
7. play
8. hay
9. gray
10. runway

Page 136: Another Long "A" Digraph

New words will vary; the following words should be circled:

1. paint
2. tail
3. rain
4. wait
5. paid
6. sail
7. stain
8. fail

Page 137: Picturing "AI" and "EI"

1. weigh
2. eight
3. train
4. sleigh
5. paint
6. chain

7–10. Sentences will vary.

Page 138: "AY" or "AI"?

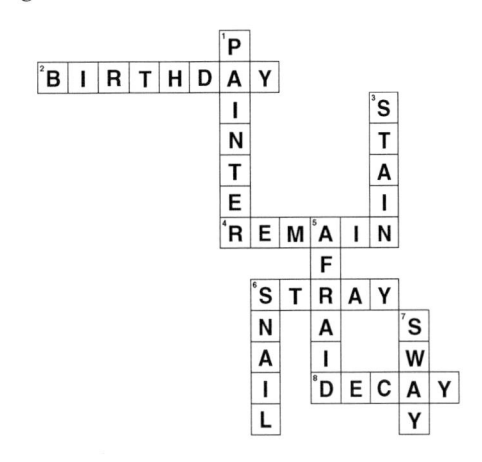

[Crossword with answers: BIRTHDAY, POINTER, STAIN, REMAIN, FAF, STRAY, NAIL, SWAY, DECAY]

Page 139: Long "A" Search

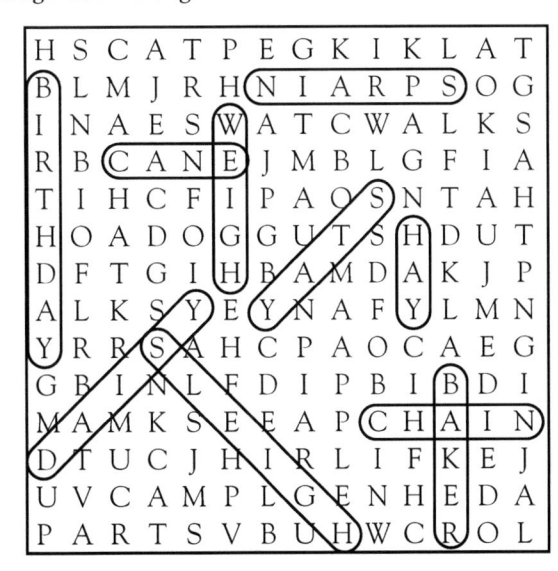

[Word search grid with circled words: PRAIN, WATCWALKS, CANE, HAY, CHAIN, etc.]

Page 140: "EY" at the End

1. b
2. d
3. h
4. e
5. a
6. f
7. c
8. g
9. survey, obey, they, Grey
10. monkey, barley, kidney, Shirley

Page 141: The Sounds of "EA"

2. ā
3. ĕ
4. ĕ
5. ē
6. ē
7. ā
8. ē
9. ĕ
10. ē
11. ĕ
12. ē

13–15. Sentences will vary.

Page 142: More on "EA"

1. seal
2. teach
3. dream
4. speak
5. bread
6. spread
7. sweat
8. break
9. great

Page 143: Long "E"
1. money
2. cream
3. hockey
4. clean
5. week
6. monkey
7. cheese
8. green
9. easy
10. agree
11. deep
12. meal

Page 144: Which Is Correct?
1. teeth
2. sheet
3. free
4. neat
5. steam
6. bleed
7. meal
8. green
9. beam
10. leaf
11. street
12. sheep
13. easy
14. keep
15. treat
16. speak
17. teeth, sheet, free, bleed, green, street, sheep, keep
18. neat, steam, meal, beam, leaf, easy, treat, speak

Page 145: Sound Alikes
1. see
2. week
3. meat
4. peak
5. tea
6. seam
7. creek
8. flea

Page 146: Long "E" Crossing

```
    ¹S
    T        ²B
    R    ³C R E E K
    E    L   A
⁴P E A C E   M
    T    ⁵S
       ⁶M O N K E Y
         E   E
       ⁷E E L
         T   D     ⁸L
             ⁹C H I M N E Y
             N       A
             G       S
                     H
```

Page 147: Two Sounds for "IE"
1. lie, pie, die, dried
2. movie, field, believe, married
3. movie
4. die
5. married
6. lie
7. dried
8. pie
9. field
10. believe

Page 148: Long "E" or Long "A"?
1. ē
2. ā
3. ē
4. ā
5. ē
6. ā
7. ē
8. ē
9. ē
10. ē
11. ē
12. ā
13. ceiling
14. protein
15. beige
16. receive
17. veil
18. caffeine

Page 149: Two Vowels—One Sound
1. grow
2. toes or tows
3. coach
4. throat
5. bowl
6. doe
7. hoe or how
8. toast
9. slow
10. bowl, oatmeal
11. toast
12. throat, swallow
13. slowly
14. tiptoed
15. road

Page 150: "OA" Sentences
1. toad, boat
2. coal
3. toaster
4. coach, goal
5. goat
6. soaking
7. coaster
8. roast
9. throat
10. cockroach

Page 151: "OW" and Long "O"
1. low, ō; bow, ō or ou; know, ō; snow, ō
2. mow, ō; blow, ō; crow, ō; show, ō
3. row, ō; throw, ō; grow, ō; flow, ō
4. Tomorrow, Halloween, snow, yellow, pillowcase, blow
5. clown, gown, crown, town, how

Page 152: Long "O" Sound

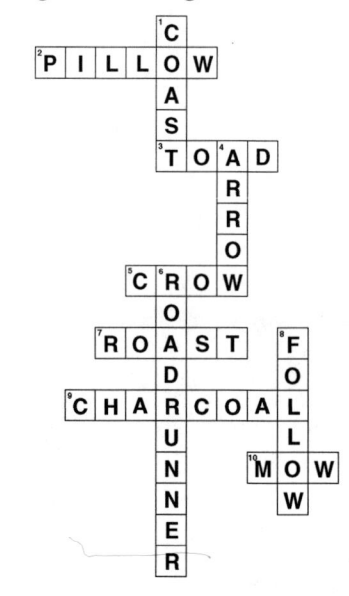

```
            ¹C
       ²P I L L O W
            A
            S
          ³T O ⁴A D
               R
               R
               O
          ⁵C ⁶R O W
            O
          ⁷R O A S T   ⁸F
            D             O
          ⁹C H A R C O A L
            U             L
            N           ¹⁰M O W
            N             W
            E
            R
```

Page 153: The Sounds of "OW"
1. g
2. j
3. i
4. h
5. d
6. e
7. f
8. c
9. b
10. a
11–13. Sentences will vary.

Daily Skill-Builders **Spelling & Phonics 4–5** **195**

Page 154: Sounds of "OU"
1. young; touch
2. pouch; cloud
3. could; would
4. you; soup
5. though; dough
6. south; cloud
7. mouse; cloud
8. poultry; dough
9. groups; soup
10. through; soup
11. shoulder; dough
12. couch; cloud

Page 155: "OU" = "OU"
1. c
2. d
3. g
4. l
5. i
6. j
7. h
8. e
9. f
10. b
11. a
12. k

13. *The following words should be circled:* outside, mound, loud, sound, cloud, south, house, hound, snout, outdoors, house, wound, mouse.

Page 156: "OW" or "OU"?
1. ground
2. shower
3. found
4. plow
5. house
6. crowded
7. pound
8. amount
9. nightgown
10. south
11. owl
12. trout
13. vowel
14. cloud
15. house
16. clown

17. Ou should be circled in each word.

Page 157: Sound of "AW"
1–4. Aw should be circled in each word.
5. e
6. a
7. g
8. i
9. j
10. h
11. f
12. c
13. d
14. b

Page 158: "AU" Sentences
1. Au should be circled in all words.
2. faucet
3. August
4. autograph
5. haunted
6. laundry
7. exhausted
8. fault
9. sauce

Page 159: The Sound of "AU" and "AW"
1. crawl
2. automobile
3. draw
4. hawk
5. claw
6. exhaust
7. August
8. haunt
9. dawn
10. straw
11. drawn
12. exhaust
13. auburn
14. faucet
15. Paul
16. Shaw

Page 160: "OI" Versus "OY"
1. toy
2. boil
3. joy
4. coin
5. royal
6. poison
7. oyster
8. point
9. toilet
10. noise
11. avoid
12. enjoy
13. oyster
14. destroy
15. choice

Page 161: "OI" and "OY"
1. choice
2. destroy
3. foil
4. joined
5. toiled
6. enjoy
7. toys
8. noise
9. soy
10. oyster

Page 162: Crossing "OY" and "OI"

```
    S O Y B E A N
    P
    J O Y F U L
  N   I
B O I L
  I
  S     P
  E N J O Y   D
    I       E
    S       S
    J O I N T
    N       R
    A V O I D
            Y
```

Page 163: "IGH" Copycat
1. c
2. d
3. i
4. b
5. g
6. h
7. e
8. j
9. a
10. f

11–14. Sentences will vary.

Page 164: Copycat "EIGH"

The following words should be circled:
weight, neighbor, eight, freight, neigh
10. eight
11. weigh
12. sleigh
13. neigh
14. eighty
15. neighborhoods

Page 165: Compound Words
1. book, case
2. nose, dive
3. life, time
4. grand, child
5. light, house
6. snow, storm
7. shore
8. bell
9. shells
10. room
11. made
12. camp

Page 166: Grandmother's Visit
1. grandmother
2. timeline
3. newspaper
4. grapevine
5. bookmark
6. grandfather
7. seashore
8. airport
9. birthday
10. afternoon
11. waterfall
12. sunset

Page 167: Contraction Time
1. c
2. e
3. b
4. a
5. f
6. d
7. he's
8. aren't
9. She'll, we'll
10. It's

Page 168: Contractions Again
1. I am; I'm
2. did not; didn't
3. You have; You've
4. was not; wasn't
5. should have; should've
6. I would; I'd
7. She is; She's
8. I have; I've
9. It is; It's
10. were not; weren't
11. could not; couldn't
12. I have; I've

Page 169: Contraction Action
1. they are
2. would not
3. does not
4. has not
5. that is
6. you have
7. should have
8. he will
9. they will
10. were not

11–16. Sentences will vary.

Page 170: More Contractions
1. couldn't
2. won't
3. she's
4. He'll
5. haven't
6. doesn't
7. You're
8. didn't

Page 171: Contraction Crossword

Page 172: That's Mine!
1. Anna's
2. class'
3. father's
4. author's
5. kittens'
6. Jeff's
7. Kim's
8. horse's
9. mechanic's
10. principal's
11. students'
12. player's

13–17. Sentences will vary.

Page 173: That's Mine, Too!
1. the boy's hat
2. the teacher's desk
3. my mother's house
4. the girls' books
5. the dog's food
6. Tim's coat
7. the school's clock
8. Sarah's hair
9. the cats' fur
10. the people's voice
11. the children's clothing
12. the teachers' lessons

Page 174: Antonyms
1. late
2. dark
3. cooked
4. stale
5. enemy
6. calm
7. refuse
8. different
9. success
10. frown
11. stop
12. inside
13. forget
14. incorrect
15. guilty

Page 175: Synonyms
1. reply
2. find
3. propose
4. mend
5. amuse
6. haste
7. select
8. comical
9. youngsters
10. courage

11. distant
12. hurry
13. exhausted
14. grateful

Page 176: They Sound the Same!
1. week, know, here
2. see, due
3. right, eight
4. road, meet
5. seems, passed
6. fair
7. We'd
8. hear, rode

Page 177: They Look the Same!
1. tear
2. second
3. story
4. rest
5. date
6. fan
7. wind
8. bark
9. ring
10. close
11. yard
12. lead

Page 178: Multiple Meanings
1. a
2. b
3. b
4. b
5. b
6. a
7. b
8. a

Page 179: Short Vowel Review
1. glass, shelf, when, blast
2. pond, crust, yell, frog
3. contest, cobweb, kitchen, pumpkin
4. muffin, happen, bunk bed, napkin
5. glass, shelf, when, blast, pond, crust, yell, frog, bunk, bed
6. contest, cobweb, kitchen, pumpkin, muffin, happen, napkin

Page 180: Long Vowel Review
1. why, no, zero, dizzy
2. poncho, fifty, open, begin
3. tulip, relax, mason, myself
4. hope, scrape, huge, hide
5. excuse, explode, clockwise, homeroom
6. inflate, unsafe, reptile, cupcake
7. tadpole, costume, trombone, inside

WALCH PUBLISHING

Share Your Bright Ideas

We want to hear from you!

Your name_____ Date_____

School name_____

School address_____

City _____State _____Zip_____Phone number (_____)_____

Grade level(s) taught_____Subject area(s) taught_____

Where did you purchase this publication?_____

In what month do you purchase a majority of your supplements?_____

What moneys were used to purchase this product?

   ___School supplemental budget   ___Federal/state funding   ___Personal

Please "grade" this Walch publication in the following areas:

   Quality of service you received when purchasing .... A B C D
   Ease of use.. A B C D
   Quality of content.. A B C D
   Page layout .... A B C D
   Organization of material .... A B C D
   Suitability for grade level .... A B C D
   Instructional value... A B C D

COMMENTS:_____
_____

What specific supplemental materials would help you meet your current—or future—instructional needs?
_____

Have you used other Walch publications? If so, which ones?_____

May we use your comments in upcoming communications?   ___Yes   ___No

Please **FAX** this completed form to **888-991-5755**, or mail it to

   Customer Service, Walch Publishing, P. O. Box 658, Portland, ME 04104-0658

We will send you a **FREE GIFT** in appreciation of your feedback. **THANK YOU!**